www.wadsworth.com

www.wadsworth.com is the World Wide Web site for Thomson Wadsworth and is your direct source to dozens of online resources.

At *www.wadsworth.com* you can find out about supplements, demonstration software, and student resources. You can also send email to many of our authors and preview new publications and exciting new technologies.

www.wadsworth.com
Changing the way the world learns®

Current Perspectives
Readings from InfoTrac® College Edition

Cyber Crime

Current Perspectives
Readings from InfoTrac® College Edition

Cyber Crime

ROGER LᴇROY MILLER
Institute for University Studies, Arlington, Texas

Australia • Canada • Mexico • Singapore • Spain
United Kingdom • United States

THOMSON
™
WADSWORTH

Current Perspectives: Readings from InfoTrac® College Edition: Cyber Crime
Roger LeRoy Miller

Editor in Chief: *Eve Howard*
Assistant Editor: *Jana Davis*
Editorial Assistant: *Jennifer Walsh*
Technology Project Manager: *Susan DeVanna*
Marketing Manager: *Terra Schultz*
Marketing Assistant: *Annabelle Yang*
Advertising Project Manager: *Stacey Purviance*
Project Manager, Editorial Production: *Brenda Ginty*
Creative Director: *Robert Hugel*

Print Buyer: *Karen Hunt*
Permissions Editor: *Sarah Harkrader*
Cover Designer: *Larry Didona*
Production Service: *Rozi Harris, Interactive Composition Corporation*
Cover Image: *Photolibrary.com/Photonica*
Cover and Text Printer: *Webcom*
Compositor: *Interactive Composition Corporation*

Printed in Canada
1 2 3 4 5 6 7 09 08 07 06 05

For more information about our products, contact us at:
Thomson Learning Academic Resource Center
1-800-423-0563

For permission to use material from this text or product, submit a request online at
http://www.thomsonrights.com.
Any additional questions about permissions can be submitted by email to
thomsonrights@thomson.com.

Library of Congress Control Number: 2004116844

ISBN 0-495-00722-6

Thomson Higher Education
10 Davis Drive
Belmont, CA 94002-3098
USA

Asia (including India)
Thomson Learning
5 Shenton Way
#01-01 UIC Building
Singapore 068808

Australia/New Zealand
Thomson Learning Australia
102 Dodds Street
Southbank, Victoria 3006
Australia

Canada
Thomson Nelson
1120 Birchmount Road
Toronto, Ontario M1K 5G4
Canada

UK/Europe/Middle East/Africa
Thomson Learning
High Holborn House
50-51 Bedford Row
London WC1R 4LR
United Kingdom

Latin America
Thomson Learning
Seneca, 53
Colonia Polanco
11560 Mexico
D.F. Mexico

Spain (including Portugal)
Thomson Paraninfo
Calle Magallanes, 25
28015 Madrid, Spain

Contents

Preface

In the words of U.S. Attorney, Patrick L. Meehan, "The crime scene of the future is going to be a computer box." The same technology that has provided almost unlimited opportunities to businesses and consumers has also been a boon for a new breed of cyber criminals. According to the U.S. Department of Justice, online identity theft, in which a victim's personal information (name, Social Security number, credit card number, and so on) is used illegally, costs 10 million targeted individuals and businesses an estimated $50 billion a year.

In 2004, reports of Internet fraud reached 38,000, quadruple the total from five years earlier. The annual number of World Wide Web child sex crimes investigated by the Federal Bureau of Investigation (FBI) has grown from 113 to over 2,500. Computer systems that control power grids, transportation networks, and financial institutions are increasingly susceptible to terrorist cyber attacks.

Indeed, when it comes to crime on the Internet, the future is now. Given the speed with which the "rules" of the Internet shift and evolve, the criminal justice community must adapt its often rigid and formal systems to meet the challenges of cyber crime. Anyone anticipating a career in criminal justice must be aware of these challenges. I have prepared this set of articles to help students gain a thorough knowledge of the issues surrounding computer-based crime in the United States and around the world.

The articles included in this reader are designed to accompany the section covering Cyber Crime in Chapter 17 of my textbook, *Criminal Justice in Action*. The articles may, in addition, be used to supplement any of the criminal justice texts published by Thomson Wadsworth.

The recent explosion of cyber crime has been dramatic, but there can be no doubt that this new form of criminal endeavor is still in its infancy. As governments and citizens increasingly come to rely on the Internet to function on a day-to-day basis, cyber thieves and terrorists will continue to find ways to take advantage of this reliance. My reader will provide students not only with an introduction to this growing field of criminal justice and law enforcement, but also with a basic understanding of the concerns that will mark the cyber crime challenge in the years ahead.

Roger LeRoy Miller

1

Cyber Crime

Cyber Threat!

Giles Trendle

Although there were no major catastrophic cyber attacks during the war on Iraq, as some had feared, an increase in hostile electronic strikes was registered during the term of the conflict. (Business & Finance).

It was more a case of cybervandalism than cyberterrorism. However, the phenomenon of cyberwar—electronic attacks via the Internet—though not employed in this instance, is increasingly recognised in government, military and business circles as a potential grave threat.

Cyber attacks raise fears that an individual or small group can, from any-where in the world, wreak havoc by defacing or 'downing' websites, spreading viruses that disrupt computer systems, or using the Internet as a direct instrument of death by taking remote control of systems operating dam flood-gates or air traffic control, for example.

Like a classic guerrilla struggle, digital warfare is a conflict of the weak against the strong, in which the weaker force probes for vulnerable points in its enemy's defences. The Achilles Heel of modern technology appears to be that no computer system can be considered totally invulnerable to being 'cracked'. Infrastructures such as power, communications, transportation and financial services rely heavily on computers and automated control systems. This puts them at risk from cyber attacks.

"Cyber Threat!" by Giles Trendle, *The Middle East,* June 2003, p. 38–42. Reprinted by permission.

A hacker interviewed prior to the war on Iraq warned that western governments and businesses should brace themselves for 'suicide cyber attacks' in the event of war. He defined a 'suicide cyber attack' as one in which the hacker sets out to cause maximum damage unhindered by any regard for being detected and caught. The hacker who issued this stark warning belongs to a group calling itself the Iron Guards, which attacked Israeli government and business sites in the first recorded Arab-Israeli cyberwar two years ago.

Talk of suicide cyber attacks may be no more than rhetorical swagger on the part of the hacker. As it is, fears that war on Iraq would dramatically increase the likelihood of a major cyberterrorist attack—defined by the US as one originating from a country on the US State Department's terror watch list—proved unfounded. Yet Internet security experts recorded an escalation of smaller cyber attacks during the war.

There were approximately 20,000 website defacements, both pro and anti-war, during the conflict, with the vast majority taking place within the first few days, according to internet security firm F-Secure. Such defacements, the online equivalent of graffiti, tend to happen regularly and are generally, less economically damaging than a computer system infected by a virus or worm.

Five UK government sites were compromised by a hacking group protesting the war with Iraq, according to Internet security company mi2g. Messages posted on the site included propaganda against US President George W. Bush, British Prime Minister Tony Blair and Israeli premier Ariel Sharon. According to mi2g, several high profile corporate targets, including Coca-Cola and Fuji Film web sites, were hit by denial-of-service attacks, in which a site is made inaccessible.

PATRIOTIC HACKING

The war on Iraq ushered in the emergence of a new trend: the pro-American counter-attack. The website of Arab satellite TV station Al Jazeera, criticised by the US for re-broadcasting Iraqi TV's footage of American PoWs, came under intermittent denial-of-service attacks amid the war. The English language Al Jazeera web site, which posted disturbing images of civilian victims, was also downed by a denial-of-service attack. A group calling itself the Patriot Freedom Cyber Force Militia claimed responsibility for these attacks.

The National Infrastructure Protection Centre (NIPC), operated by the FBI, cautioned pro-US hackers against engaging in "patriotic hacking", raising the possibility that the United States is worried about setting a precedent for a form of warfare against which it would itself be extremely vulnerable. It is, however, widely assumed that the Joint Task Force-Computer Network Operations (JTF-CNO), created by the US Strategic Command to handle network defence and attack, engaged in hacking and electronic warfare against Iraq's telecommunications and information infrastructure. However, the Department of Defence refuses to provide any details.

GOVERNMENT RESPONSE

The US authorities are increasingly treating the potential threat of cyber attacks as a clear and present danger. The IT proficiency of militant Islamic hackers was recognised by American officials who admitted last year that they had underestimated the amount of attention Al Qaeda was paying to the Internet. "Al Qaeda spent more time mapping our vulnerabilities in cyberspace than we previously thought," confirmed Roger Cressey, the chief of staff of the White House critical infrastructure protection board, in an interview with the Washington Post last year. "The question is a question of when, not if."

Last December President Bush signed into law the E-Government Act of 2002, which is aimed at ensuring the security of online information. The law allocates $345m to e-government security initiatives over the next four years.

In Britain, the National Infrastructure Security Co-ordination Centre (NISCC) has the task of protecting the UK's critical national infrastructure—such as power, telecommunications and transportation—from electronic attack. An interdepartmental organisation created by the Home Secretary in 1999, NISCC says it is keeping the threat of digital attack under constant review.

A spokesman at NISCC recognised that, as with any other technologically advanced society, the UK's critical national infrastructure is "increasingly vulnerable" to electronic attacks, though he added that nothing suggested a risk of widespread and disruptive electronic attack following the military campaign against Iraq.

The spokesman said hackers "may be motivated to carry out less sophisticated attacks such as website defacements or denial of service attacks, but that is not in the remit of NISCC." In other words, there may possibly be more digital attacks, but scope of target remains limited and the level of skill and efficacy of such attacks remains questionable.

The office of the e-Envoy to the UK government also stressed it was taking the issue of cyber threat seriously. "We believe that we are building adequate security measures into our services, but no-one can afford to be complacent," said a spokesman for the e-Envoy. American officials seem more ready to conceive (even predict) the possibility of a devastating and catastrophic attack by cyberterrorists. The former White House advisor for cyberspace security referred to the possibility of a 'digital Pearl Harbour'. British cyber-officials, on the other hand, maintain a more reserved tone than their American counterparts which may well be due to a difference in cultural expression rather than any lower standard of professional diligence.

TARGETING THE ECONOMY

Statements by Islamic militants since the 11 September 2001 attacks indicate their growing realisation that the economy is the soft underbelly of US global power. The Internet could yet be the launching pad for future attacks on corporate targets aimed at creating economic damage in the form of business interruption, data theft, reputation loss and share price decline.

The Iron Guards hacker justifies attacks on the western corporate world by arguing that a powerful economy helps generate the capital required to wage war abroad. "We believe the West is ruled not by democracy but by capital," said the hacker. "Money funds election campaigns, controls the media, and buys weapons. Western companies help create that money and so, in this sense, we regard them as decision-makers as important as Bush and Blair."

There is uncertainty about how well-prepared businesses might be for an escalation of cyber attacks on IT systems. In a recently-published survey, the Department of Trade and Industry found that 70% of British companies were either 'not very' or 'not at all' concerned by the threat of politically-motivated attacks.

Some experts feel that, in the present climate, creating hysteria can be as much of a sin as complacency. Hackers can be anonymous, nebulous and elusive. Such a threat, because it is unseen, creates uncertainty and where there is uncertainty there is room for fear and fear-mongering. "I think the media overplays the hype associated with cyberterrorism," says Clifford May, chief forensic consultant at Integralis, a British IT security company. "Large companies may be attractive targets but they have very strong security in place."

Hacking comes under what military theorists refer to as 'asymmetric' (uneven) warfare, in which unconventional tactics are sought by the weaker side to counter the overwhelming superiority of an adversary. Cyberterrorism might prove to be attractive to extremist groups looking for a more level playing field on which to fight. And cyberspace may emerge as an accurate barometer of geopolitical tensions worldwide—the greater the tension, the greater the number of cyber attacks.

The much-feared, massive cyberterrorist attack did not materialise during the war on Iraq. Yet there is no room for holding illusions of invulnerability or relying on what has, or has not, happened in the past as an indicator of what will happen in the future. Constant vigilance and a heightened security awareness—backed up by the IT tools to detect and prevent electronic attacks or incursions—continue to be the way forward.

2

Crime and the Internet

Schemers Flourish on Web's Seedy Side

Jenni Bergal and Purva Patel

The Internet can be a great tool: It can help friends across the world communicate; it can seek out cheap travel deals; it can educate patients about prescription drugs.

But there's another side of the Web, one that schemers such as con artists and pedophiles have latched onto, drawing victims into the darkest caverns of cyberspace and leaving law enforcement agencies scrambling to keep up.

Internet scams, child pornography sites and cyber-stalking are all part of the seedy side of the Web.

"Internet fraud is a booming business. It's a relatively easy and inexpensive way to reach out and rob people," said Susan Grant, director of the National Fraud Information Center/Internet Fraud Watch, an arm of the National Consumers League in Washington, D.C. Last year, victims lost $122 million in Internet-related fraud schemes, according to a Federal Trade Commission database that gathers complaints from federal, state and local law enforcement agencies and private organizations such as Better Business Bureaus. That represented 47 percent of all fraud complaints—up from 31 percent just two years earlier.

"Internet fraud is a big problem. Partly, it's a translation of schemes that existed offline forever," said Eric A. Wenger, an attorney in the FTC's bureau

"Schemers Flourish on Web's Seedy Side" by Jenni Bergal and Purva Patel, *South Florida Sun-Sentinel*, Dec. 1, 2003. Reprinted with permission from the *South Florida Sun-Sentinel*.

of consumer protection in Washington. "It's an easy way to reach out to lots of people, because the costs are so low and you can operate 24 hours a day."

Authorities say perpetrators of fraud love using the Internet, because they can send out millions of e-mails to potential victims at a minimal cost. They say it's quicker and easier to create and shut down a Web site than to open and close a boiler room filled with salespeople. Among the most common "dot-cons": online auctions, in which scammers offer items they don't have or misrepresent what they're selling; computer equipment scams, in which victims order merchandise and never get it; and bogus offers of loans and credit cards, which require victims to pay fees upfront.

Other popular scams use e-mail to pitch phony sweepstakes or bogus health and diet products, such as pills that claim to help people lose weight without dieting or exercise, or products that "cure" impotence or hair loss.

Authorities say South Florida has become a hot spot for Internet con artists, just as it's been home to traditional boiler rooms for decades.

"More fraud cases originate from South Florida and L.A. than from other parts of the country," said the FTC's Wenger.

Take the case of William Caudell, who cheated 48,000 investors from around the world out of more than $13 million in an Internet business opportunity scam, according to court records.

Caudell was founder and CEO of Professional Resource Systems International, a Boca Raton, Fla.-based company that used the Internet to offer customers a nonexistent e-commerce opportunity for $295 a person. The company promised customers that an electronic "store" would provide them a way to engage in e-commerce through electric retailing of goods and services on a pornography-free "Internet mall."

But authorities said there was no mall Web site and the operation was a scam. Caudell pleaded guilty to conspiracy to launder money and commit mail and wire fraud and was sentenced last year to 11 years in federal prison and ordered to pay almost $13.6 million in restitution.

While authorities didn't have a problem tracking down Caudell, sometimes it's hard for them to pinpoint where an Internet scam is based, because of the global nature of the Internet.

"A perpetrator in Brazil can hack into a system in the United States, routing his attack via several other countries, obtain evidence from the U.S. system, such as a bank, and extort money," said Susan Brenner, a University of Dayton (Ohio) law professor and co-chairwoman of the National Institute of Justice's Electronic Crime Partnership Initiative. "The circuitous path the perpetrator follows makes it much, much more difficult for law enforcement to find him . . . So, there is little, if any, risk of being apprehended. This is a completely new experience."

One of the biggest and longest running worldwide frauds is the "Nigerian letter scam," which has evolved from mail to fax to the Internet and is still going strong. In this scheme, an unsolicited e-mail marked "confidential" or "urgent" arrives, often claiming that a top government official or bank officer in Nigeria or another West African country has amassed millions of dollars and needs to transfer it overseas. This person asks victims to put the millions into their bank accounts for safekeeping and offers a 10 percent to 35 percent cut for their help, then requests money upfront for miscellaneous expenses or processing fees.

The Web's cloak of anonymity not only helps fraud artists, it has led other types of criminals to become more brazen. Some pedophiles send out pornographic material over the Internet to children or have sexually explicit conversations with them, hoping to tempt a youngster into a sexual act. Experts say child porn sites are proliferating and the number of pedophiles using them has grown exponentially as more people grow comfortable with technology.

"The Internet is like a giant playground for pedophiles and predators," said Nancy McBride, director of prevention education at the West Palm Beach office of the Alexandria, Va.-based National Center for Missing and Exploited Children. "Since there's a sense of anonymity, they feel very powerful."

Since 1996, the FBI has obtained 2,947 convictions related to child pornography on the Internet and online crimes against children.

"It's out of control," said Bob Breeden, a supervisor at the Florida Department of Law Enforcement's computer crimes center in Tallahassee. "Parents have no idea, if they're not paying attention, how readily available children are to pedophiles on the Internet."

In September, a Davie, Fla., dentist was sentenced to almost six years in prison for attempting to lure a minor into sexual activity via the Internet using the screen name Rendezvous777.

Prosecutors said Joseph Messier, 28, had a long, sexually explicit online chat with an undercover U.S. Secret Service agent who he thought was a 13-year-old girl. Messier arranged to meet the girl later that night in back of a grocery store in Miami. Investigators caught him outside the store with condoms and other sexual aids in his car.

His attorney, Michael Hursey, said Messier maintains his innocence and is appealing his conviction.

Cyberspace also makes it easier for people to engage in stalking and harassment, experts say. Cyber stalking can range from sending threatening, obscene or hateful e-mail to spreading vicious rumors about others online to electronic sabotage, such as overwhelming a computer system with thousands of e-mails.

There are no government statistics documenting the frequency of cyberstalking, but experts say the numbers are growing.

Stalkers target people they know, strangers and even companies, and their online anonymity can make the experience scary for victims, said Brenner of the Electronic Crime Partnership Initiative.

"Online you don't know who it is or who they are," Brenner said. "They could be halfway across the world or across the street."

3

Online Auction Fraud

Bitten Bidders

Jodie Kirshner

Bitten bidders. (victims of online auction fraud)

Last month, Michael Snyder, an artistic director at a record label in San Francisco, spotted an incredible deal on eBay for a laptop computer—50 percent below retail. A savvy shopper, Snyder reasoned that failing dot coms all over the Bay Area were liquidating their equipment at bargain prices. He reviewed the seller's "feedback," a record of comments from other customers, and checked the product's specifications and warranty. "It was certainly a glamorous offer, A+ across the board," he recalls.

The seller said he was on assignment in Spain, but Snyder was hungry to get the deal. So he arranged to wire money to a Spanish friend who could buy the computer in person, as a precaution. But the seller insisted on having the wire transfer tracking number. Hours later, the seller arrived in a Western Union office with the number, posing as Snyder's friend. "I've taken your money," he later E-mailed Snyder. And he attached this after-the-fact warning: "You should be more careful buying things on the Internet."

Indeed, he should. According to the Federal Trade Commission, auction scams are now the most prevalent type of Internet fraud. In 2002, the agency received 51,000 online auction complaints, up from roughly 20,000 the previous year. Authorities say even these figures fail to capture the enormity of the problem. Not only is the occurrence of auction fraud greater than the number

---

of cases reported, but the types of fraud committed have grown increasingly complicated.

CONVOLUTED

"While we used to see stories about people who would not send an item as described, send broken items, or not deliver at all, frauds are just getting much more sophisticated than that," says Ina Steiner, editor of AuctionBytes.com, an online resource for Internet auction buyers and sellers. Con artists have turned to online auction sites as a hunting ground for new victims, luring people off the sites, posting illegitimate ads, or sending spoof E-mails to trick them. They have even used identity theft to avoid detection.

The vast majority of online auction fraud occurs on eBay, simply because it is the biggest auction site, says Shawn Hutton, research associate at the National White Collar Crime Center. EBay, based in San Jose, Calif., boasted roughly 69 million registered users worldwide through March 31 this year and $1.2 billion of net revenue in 2002. Nearly 8 million bids are placed every day. Spokesperson Kevin Pursglove says that fraud is minimal but concedes it is hard to track.

Still, officials say the dollar amounts of the scams are growing in tandem with their complexity. In April, the U.S. attorney in Massachusetts announced the sentencing of Teresa Smith, 25, the perpetrator of the largest Internet auction scheme ever prosecuted: Approximately 300 bidders were defrauded of $857,776 in computer equipment purchases. "I still get a sick feeling in my stomach every time I think about the money I lost to her," says Dave Curry, a Doylestown, Pa., schoolteacher who lost $2,335. Curry was luckier than some. Earlier this year, Robert Jaramillo and Alexander Sajid Hipkins, posing as BMW sellers, lured bidders to New Mexico. The two were indicted for conspiring to take the money by force once the victim arrived. They have entered plea agreements and one has already been sentenced.

Online auction fraud is difficult for authorities to investigate, and victims rarely recover the money they have lost. "It's not like hopping in a police car and questioning witnesses, and zero to none would be my estimation of how often people recover their losses," says Hutton. Frequently, victims believe the online auction site should solve their problems and fail to report crimes to the correct authorities. In reality, online auction sites are fairly powerless once a crime has occurred.

Often, customers are the ones bringing fraud to investigators' attention. That happened in Nevada, where Orlando Zamora allegedly posed as a jewelry buyer, contacting eBay sellers whose auctions had not been successful. Zamora offered to buy the baubles if the sellers would remove the items from eBay and use a particular escrow service. Orlando's wife, says Nevada Deputy Attorney General Robert Griffy, then masqueraded as an escrow service employee, contacting the seller and pretending that money had been deposited in the account so it was OK to send the jewelry. "We only found out about this when one customer did some research and discovered that the escrow service didn't have any offices in the United States," says Griffy.

The FTC is hoping to crack down harder on such scams, and in April launched "Operation Bidder Beware." But Delores Gardner Thompson, an attorney in the FTC's Division of Marketing Practices, cautions that consumers are still often in the best position to protect themselves. She recommends that online auction-goers act like gumshoes before placing a bid. They should confirm the seller's address, telephone number, and perhaps even match phone numbers with addresses on reverse directories.

The same Internet that provides fraudsters with anonymity, also provides users with tools for tracking down people. Some victims are forming their own "rings" to help others on the Internet fight fraud. After trying to buy a laptop computer, Dale Peterson, an architect and construction manager in New York, discovered an online forum devoted to the seller who took his money and ran. The forum participants—victims like Peterson—tracked the seller to North Carolina, not Atlanta where the seller had purported to operate a company. Another victim used an online reverse directory to determine the seller's true identity. Armed with a name, Peterson then downloaded court documents about the seller—turns out this wasn't his first go-round with cheating—and posted them on the Internet to help other victims.

On May 13, the perpetrator was arrested and charged with wire and mail fraud. Several members of the online forum plan to attend the sentencing hearing in Asheville, N.C., where they will meet in person for the first time. "We wanted to see justice done for the person who stole from us," says Peterson.

DETECTIVE WORK

Trouble Ahead

Before bidding, learn the signs of an online auction scam:

LOCATION, LOCATION. Be wary of an item listed for sale in the United States but later revealed to be from overseas. Dealing with overseas sellers is risky, as it can be tough for U.S. law enforcement to prosecute international cases. Don't send money to addresses not listed in the original ad.

ESCROW WATCH. Avoid online escrow services that require users to set up accounts with online payment services. Escrow services are in the business of taking money and should be equipped to do so themselves. Online escrow services should also not claim to comply with the "U.S. Financial and Business Code." No such code exists.

NOTHING'S THAT CHEAP. Too-low prices can be a sign something's amiss. Check stores and price comparison sites for realistic prices.

AVOID STRANGERS. Be wary of buyers and sellers who try to lure customers away from auction sites with promises of better deals.

DON'T TELL. Auctions are not confessionals. Don't disclose sensitive information without knowing why it's being collected, how it will be used, and how it will be protected. Don't respond to threats that accounts will be terminated unless such details are provided.

PUSH PLASTIC. The safest way to pay is by credit card, as your issuer provides charge-back protections. Beware of sellers who say they accept credit cards but reveal later that the buyer must use his credit card to do a wire transfer; such transfers have no safeguards.

For more information, consult the following online resources:
FEDERAL TRADE COMMISSION
www.ftc.gov
Get more tips on avoiding a bad auctioneer. INTERNET FRAUD COMPLAINT CENTER
www.ifccfbi.gov
Your complaint will be forwarded to the appropriate law enforcement authorities.

4

Online Retail Fraud

Latest Internet Scam Goes After the Good-Hearted

Richard Espinoza and Dan Margolies

KANSAS CITY, Mo.—An Internet scam that preys not on the greedy but on the good-hearted has started draining thousands of dollars from bank accounts in Kansas and Missouri.

Many Internet scams rely on victims' avarice to draw them in. The new scam depends instead on people's ignorance of obscure banking rules and their desire to return money that is not theirs.

It recently cost a Shawnee, Mo., man $74,500.

The scheme is too new for law enforcement officials to have a handle on how many people it has snared. A handful of cases in the two states suggest a steady stream of victims. In Overland Park, Kan., last month, a man who was selling a motorcycle lost $1,350. A victim in Topeka, Kan., lost $42,000. A third in Hannibal, Mo., lost $5,500.

But the hardest hit was the 38-year-old Shawnee man, stung after he posted a car for sale on the Internet for $17,500.

Someone agreed to buy the car and sent what appeared to be a $92,000 cashier's check to the man's credit union, according to a police report.

Then the con artist told the seller that his secretary had sent the wrong check and asked him to send the extra $74,500 back. The story sounded fishy to the Shawnee man, so he said he would wire the money back to the buyer's account in the United Kingdom, but only after the cashier's check had cleared.

The victim, who spoke on condition of anonymity, said CommunityAmerica Credit Union told him the check cleared by April 29, so he wired the money out of his account. On May 8 the credit union told the Shawnee man the cashier's check had turned out to be a worthless counterfeit.

He was on the hook for more than $74,000. "They're claiming that if they can't get the funds recalled, I'm liable," the man said last week. "In light of the circumstances, I think I've got a good chance to fight it . . . I went on the faith that they (the credit union) are doing their job."

A CommunityAmerica spokeswoman referred questions to police and, citing privacy concerns, declined to say whether the credit union would hold the man responsible for the loss. If it does, the man said, he might be forced into bankruptcy.

If the scam's short history is an indication, victims should not count on anyone to bail them out after a wire transfer.

"The key with the wire is, once it's gone, it's gone," said Vince Wagner, a risk management expert with credit union service provider CUNA Mutual Group. "If they (financial institutions) follow your instructions, they're no longer liable."

The scam, which officials first noticed last summer, takes advantage of a federal rule requiring financial institutions to make money available within days, even for transactions that have not officially cleared.

The Federal Deposit Insurance Corp. requires banks to make money from cashier's, certified or teller's checks available in one to five days. But a well-made counterfeit check can bounce around the financial system for two weeks before anyone realizes it is worthless. That leaves plenty of time for a victim to wire thousands of dollars to a con artist who cashes out and vanishes.

Banking officials say people need to find out whether transactions actually cleared the issuing institution before they use the money.

The attorneys general of Missouri, Kansas and Iowa started warning people about the scam in February.

"Even the most skeptical consumer can be deceived," Iowa Attorney General Tom Miller said in a news release. "First, the checks are superb facsimiles—counterfeit, but so authentic that they often fool bank personnel who study them. Second, people think the cashier's check must be good when the bank gives them the money—especially if they insist they are skeptical, as many victims do."

Bill Hoyt, a public information officer for Kansas Attorney General Phill Kline, said he was impressed with one counterfeit cashier's check he saw this year.

It was printed on expensive paper and bore a security watermark. The job was so good, he said, he wondered whether it also was printed with the magnetic, machine-readable ink that banks use on real checks.

"These checks are first-class. They're really professionally done," Hoyt said. "Your own banks aren't going to know it's counterfeit."

Law enforcement and finance officials think that whether victims send wire transfers to Europe, Africa or elsewhere outside the United States, the money ends up with the same people, who run what authorities call the Nigerian scam.

If you have an e-mail box, chances are good you have heard recently from the widow or nephew of a fallen African potentate seeking your help in exchange for millions of dollars. People who fall for the scam can find their accounts wiped clean.

"It's the same huge gang of perpetrators, but they're using new tricks," Miller said.

Also known as advance fee fraud or 419 fraud, after a section of the Nigerian penal code, the pitch promises the recipient 30 percent or more of a multimillion-dollar sum.

The writer offers to transfer an "overinvoiced contract" or other money to the recipient's personal bank account.

In return, the recipient is asked to provide his or her bank account number and other personal information. Official-looking documents vouch for the proposal's authenticity. Eventually the recipient is asked to provide advance fees for taxes, attorney's fees, transfer taxes, performance bonds and sometimes even bribes.

If the recipient takes the bait, "complications" will arise, necessitating additional payments. Eventually, the recipient's bank account is cleaned out.

Consider the case of Pueblo, Colo., lawyer Kirk P. Brown, who was contacted in November 1995 by a person claiming to be a Nigerian citizen representing a Nigerian construction firm.

As recounted in a decision last week by the 10th U.S. Circuit Court of Appeals, the person told Brown that the Nigerian government owed his firm $21 million as payment for building a major oil pipeline.

He further told Brown that the government was looking for an offshore account in which to deposit the money, as well as an escrow agent to settle claims.

Brown, through a company he operated, agreed to become the escrow agent. In return, he was to get part of the proceeds deposited in the escrow account.

But first he would have to pay a "stamp duty," a "bond fee," "exchange rate levies" and later a "handling fee."

Because he did not have enough money to pay all the costs himself, Brown recruited investors. All told, Brown coughed up $700,000 in fees, of which $500,000 came from the investors.

The proceeds from the construction project never found their way into the escrow account. The irate investors sued Brown, the government of Nigeria and the Central Bank of Nigeria under the Racketeer Influenced and Corrupt Organizations Act.

The Nigerian government claimed sovereign immunity. Although the victims contended that they could sue under a "commercial activity" exception to the doctrine, a lower court held otherwise, and the 10th Circuit agreed.

Like many of the victims of the Nigerian scam and its new variations, Brown, who did not return phone calls seeking comment, is out of luck. So if you happen to get an e-mail from Joe-Daniels Koffi of Lome, Togo, in west Africa offering you a share of $35 million in overinvoiced proceeds, authorities recommend you do the sensible thing: Delete it.

Be extremely skeptical if someone "overpays" you by a large amount.

If you receive a cashier's check, make sure it has cleared the issuing bank before you refund any money. If the check is a counterfeit, money from it might be available in your account for two weeks before the bank realizes the check is bogus.

If you are a scam victim, call the U.S. Secret Service at (202) 406-5572 or write to U.S. Secret Service, Financial Crimes Division, 950 H St. NW, Washington, DC 20223. Also, call your state attorney general's consumer protection division.

5

Cyber Theft

Getting Personal

Elizabeth Millard

Getting personal: identity thieves are everywhere. But the good guys are, too.
(IT Security)

Although identity theft has gotten a wealth of attention over the last few years, the problem is far from gone. In actuality, the threat is growing, to the point where anyone who shops, surfs, or works online needs to be more vigilant than ever.

The ease of online transactions is attractive to individuals and companies alike. Who hasn't appreciated being able to pay a bill at 3 a.m., regardless of whether they've actually done it or not? Unfortunately, this quick and easy access to online records has its downside in identity theft. Often, the crime is only discovered when a bank account is suddenly empty or numerous credit card accounts are opened and maxed out. Last year, 10 million Americans were victims of identity theft, an increase of 41 percent over the previous year.

"It's the fastest-growing crime," says James Van Dyke, founder and principal analyst of San Francisco-based Javelin Strategy and Research. "I think consumers still have no idea how widespread it is."

SNEAK THIEVES

As technology becomes more prevalent and sophisticated, so do hackers and other miscreants who see tech as an entryway for fraud. One of the newest threats is called phishing—basically, a bad guy creates a Web site that looks as if it's part of a legitimate financial institution, like Citibank. Often, the site is a pop-up window that piggybacks on the real site. Then, he sends out thousands of spam messages telling consumers that they have to re-register with Citibank due to a security upgrade, or another seemingly mundane reason.

Because the link inside the e-mail is a trusted one, like www.citibank.com, the person clicks through, sees the legitimate site and the pop-up window, and assumes they're related. After some entry of personal info like a Social Security number and a credit card number, Mr. Responsible Consumer becomes one of the thousands who've gotten scammed by the technique.

Dave Jevans, chairman of the Anti-Phishing Working Group, says that the problem is increasingly serious. Worse, these aren't just kids who know their way around a broadband connection.

"It's pretty clear that organized crime is involved," Jevans says. "Because of where it's coming from, like eastern Russia, and the fact that the FBI is really involved in watching this, makes it evident that this international cybercrime at its peak."

The FBI is concerned that phishers are using the ill-gotten money to fund terrorism. There'd be plenty to use—phishers can make 10 times more money with the fake Web site method than they would be hacking into company servers or spying on e-mail.

The identity thieves of yesteryear are still around as well. Usually termed dumpster divers, these are people who dig through trash outside of a house or company, hoping for records that show Social Security numbers or bank information. Since they're technologically savvy, these divers have also learned that old computer equipment can still hold information, even if it seems like everything's been erased.

NEW WEAPONS

The news that identity theft is growing so quickly might be enough to make someone want to pack up and head for an unwired cabin in the hills, but there's good news to go with the bad. First, there's been recognition of the problem by legislators as well as by financial institutions. Such an overwhelming amount of fraud has the potential to cripple banks and credit card companies—and to frighten congressmen as well.

The Anti-Phishing Working Group is just one of many organizations that have made the issue into a crusade. Sites like Identity Theft 911 www.identitytheft911.com and Identity Theft Resource Center www.idtheftcenter.org have numerous resources for individuals who are trying to prevent theft, or need information on what to do if they've become a victim. Perhaps the most important step toward limiting identity theft is coming from financial institutions like Citibank, US Bank, and Wells Fargo. This makes a great deal of sense, given how much these companies have to lose. Citibank in particular has tried to attack the problem with television ads, notices on its Web site, and policies that protect cardholders if they become victims of the crime.

With legislation, organization, and better protection from banks and credit card companies, there's a possibility that identity theft can finally be minimized. But that will only happen if consumers become educated, and work to protect themselves, says John Movina, spokesperson for the Coalition Against Unsolicited Email.

"At the end of the day, user education is the only thing that works long-term," Movina notes. "You can create technical blocks and try to enact legislation that will limit the damage, but to prevent it from happening in the first place, you have to have an educated consumer who doesn't fall for the tricks and scams in the first place."

RELATED ARTICLE: KEEP IT TO YOURSELF

Getting a credit card bill for a vacation you never took shouldn't be your first introduction to identity theft. Here are some ways to lessen the risk that your info will be stolen:

- Before throwing out computer equipment like hard drives or disks, make sure to erase data properly. Simply throwing electronic documents in the "trash" doesn't mean the information isn't on your computer anymore. Invest in a software program like the BPS Data Shredder www.sofotex.com/BPS-Data-Shredder-download_L17215.html that destroys documents, even if they're in locked folders.

- If you get an e-mail from your bank or credit card company asking you for information in order to adhere to new security standards, or for any other reason, don't give it out. Even if the site link in the e-mail looks legitimate, it's probably from a phisher who has built a dummy site. If you're not sure if it's real, call the company.

- Surf on legitimate sites, and give your information out sparingly. If a small-time shopping site needs your social security number as "confirmation," it's time to take your business elsewhere.

- When doing online shopping, don't use a public e-mail account like Hotmail or Yahoo to receive records of your transactions. Accounts like these are notoriously insecure, and horror stories abound about hackers reading the e-mail of Hotmail users.

6

Cyber Consumer Fraud

Gone Phishing

Jim Middlemiss

Gone Phishing: in the latest identity-theft scam, fraudulent e-mails trick individuals into coughing up passwords to 'secure' financial data. (Identity Theft)

WHEN THE SEC swooped in on Oak Grove, Ky., resident K.C. Smith last year, the 20-year-old was accused of creating a number of fake Web sites in a year-long scheme that bilked investors of $102,000. Among other accusations, the SEC said that Smith created and maintained a fictitious Web site for the Maryland Investment Club that claimed to offer investors double-digit returns and promised that "every dime you invest is 100 percent guaranteed."

The SEC charged that Smith sent out a total of nine million spam e-mails soliciting investors. He concealed his identity from investors, the SEC said, by using disposable cellular phones, accessing the Internet through stolen ISP accounts and using online payment services that provide confidentiality. Without admitting or denying the allegations, Smith agreed in May 2003 to a disgorgement order that required him to pay $107,510.

While elaborate, the Smith scheme is not unusual. The latest Internet scam is "phishing," where scammers use e-mails to "fish" for passwords and financial data from unsuspecting consumers. "It's becoming a huge problem, and we're almost to the point where I am tempted to say if you haven't been phished yet, you will be," says Wayne Abernathy, assistant secretary of the U.S. Treasury.

A typical phishing campaign, Abernathy explains, features e-mails that direct recipients to a fraudulent Web site that resembles a legitimate organization's site. The consumer is asked to update sensitive personal data that the thieves then use to commit fraud, he continues. According to the Anti-Phishing Working Group, an industry association formed to combat fraud, there were 1,197 unique phishing attacks in May alone, and financial-services firms were the top target. (Citibank was the organization most targeted, with 370 attacks.)

Stamford, Conn.-based research firm Gartner reports that more than 57 million Americans have likely received a fraudulent e-mail, and direct losses from such identity theft cost financial institutions $1.2 billion last year. Avivah Litan, vice president and research director at Gartner, says that 19 percent of those who receive a phishing attack (about 11 million Americans) will click through to the link of the spoofed site provided in the e-mail. About 3 percent actually provide their personal information. "Phishing attack victims are almost three times as prone to identity-theft-related fraud as other online consumers. Financial institutions, Internet service providers and other service providers need to take phishing seriously," he says.

OPPORTUNITY KNOCKS

The crooks are quick to act when opportunities arise. When Royal Bank Financial Group experienced a computer glitch in June that resulted in thousands of clients not receiving their automatic pay deposits, fraudsters quickly hit the Internet with an e-mail and spoofing campaign, urging recipients to cough up passwords and personal data or risk having their accounts suspended. Royal was forced to issue a fraud alert.

But the true damage done by phishing attacks is difficult to measure. Few financial-services firms are willing to speak on the record, and those contacted for this story declined to comment or indicated phishing wasn't a problem for them. Still, one thing is clear: Phishing is more of a problem for banks than brokerages, at least for the moment.

To understand how prevalent the problem is, the Financial Services Technology Consortium (www.fstc.org), which is comprised of North American-based financial institutions, technology vendors, independent research organizations and government agencies, has launched a counter-phishing initiative. "The issue certainly doesn't seem to be going away," says Jim Salters, director, technology initiatives and project development, who adds that phishing is simply an evolution of the types of fraud that financial institutions have always faced.

A 15-page project proposal available on the FSTC Web site notes that "Phishing is clearly a significant concern for financial institutions. From a risk-assessment perspective, it has the character and current potential to create significant operational and reputational risks."

Under the plan, the FSTC proposes to launch a three-phase project to examine and possibly introduce counter-phishing initiatives. Phase one is the knowledge-acquisition and options-development stage; phase two focuses on implementation of pilot and test projects and will provide recommendations for action; and phase three will include dynamic monitoring and updating of tools and countermeasures. Salters says the FSTC hopes to launch the project this fall and "understand the issue by year end."

INSECURE SECURITIES

Though the problem currently seems confined to banks, brokerages aren't impervious to attacks. John Reed Stark, chief of the Office of Internet Enforcement at the SEC, says the attacks in the securities industry are more along the lines of what he calls "phishing derivatives."

For example, one offender, Van T. Dinh, was sentenced to 13 months in jail and ordered to pay restitution after he broke into a TD Waterhouse investor's account and exercised options trades that cut his losses on a failed investment. The perpetrator got the investor's ID information thanks to a program that the investor unwittingly downloaded onto his computer after Dinh urged fellow investors in an online chat room to check out some software he had developed.

In addition, Reed Stark says there have been some instances of "schemes orchestrated offshore designed to defraud investors," which the SEC is investigating. "I can't say for sure if there are any instances where somebody has hijacked a legitimate brokerage firm Web site," he concedes. "We want to be really careful. We don't want to overstate or understate the problem." According to Reed Stark, the SEC has set up an e-mail address for complaints about enforcement issues, and it receives 1,300 e-mails a day. "Internet users are very good at finding a place to complain," he says.

Assistant Treasury Secretary Abernathy says, "It's good news that nobody has hit [brokerages] yet. It's bad news if they think they're invulnerable. They need to take the opportunity to prepare and defend themselves." He speculates that one of the reasons why criminals might be targeting banks over brokerages is that "crooks are more aware of banks than they are of brokerage institutions." But it's only a matter of time. "Once [criminals] figure out they can go the brokerage route, I can see them doing that."

RELATED ARTICLE: TACKLE TIPS
FOR PHISHING

To fight phishing attacks, The U.S. Treasury Department has issued a report on how to avoid becoming a victim. The report suggests that financial institutions:

- Personalize e-mails to consumers.
- Keep their Web site certificates up to date.

- Remind customers to load the latest security patches.
- Provide a phone number on their Web sites that consumers can contact to verify e-mail requests.
- Register domain names that are similar to their own.
- Establish a trademark for the domain names of the firm. They should also monitor use of their trademarks and Web content and watch for spoofed sites.

If a firm becomes a victim, it should:

- Promptly issue an alert to consumers.
- Advise consumers by e-mail not to respond to suspicious e-mails.
- Alert staff and third-party vendors.
- Advise victims to change their passwords.
- Contact the ISP hosting the illegitimate site and request it be shut down immediately.
- Contact a law enforcement agency.

7

Cyberstalking

As Stalkers Go Online, New State Laws Try to Catch Up

Terry Costlow

As stalkers go online, new state laws try to catch up: One of the first trials for 'cyberstalking' in the US opens in Illinois this week. (USA)

CHICAGO—Angela Moubray used to love her hobby of chatting about wrestling and soap operas with others in an Internet chat room at night. Then, one day, a regular participant sent her a menacing e-mail. And then another. Soon, she says, he barraged her with a stream of threats such as "I hope you get raped."

Over nearly two years, the Virginia resident received unrelenting messages from a person whom she had never met, culminating in the missive: "I will kill you Ang, I mean it."

Angela Moubray is one of a growing number of people who have become a victim of an emerging new crime—cyberstalking. Upwards of 100 new cases are reported each week of someone using the Internet to intimidate another person.

"Probably two-thirds of the cases involve revenge; someone loses an argument or is turned down romantically," says Colin Hatcher, president of SafetyEd, one of a handful of private groups that help victims of Internet stalking.

"As Stalkers Go Online, New State Laws Try to Catch Up," by Terry Costlow, *Christian Science Monitor,* Sept. 3, 2002, p. 2. Reprinted by permission of the author.

Despite the prevalence of such incidents, arrests are rare. This week, however, one of the first cases of cyberstalking in the US will be played out in a suburban Chicago courtroom. The trial offers a window into how difficult such cases are to prosecute, but also signals that authorities are beginning to take the crime seriously.

All but six states have cyberstalking statutes on the books, but the Illinois case is "one of very few arrests I've heard of," says Jayne Hitchcock, president of Working to Halt Online Abuse (WHOA).

Legislators and policemen acknowledge the seriousness of the problem, but more pressing offenses often force them to overlook a crime that can be time-consuming to prosecute. Not to mention difficult. The global nature of the Internet means that the culprit could live in another state or country, and is unlikely to be extradited for what's usually a misdemeanor.

The Illinois case is the state's first arrest for cyberstalking since a statute was passed a year ago. Profirios Liapis scheduled to go on trial this week for allegedly e-mailing death threats to another man. Police say that Mr. Liapis—who could face three years in prison if convicted—is a former boyfriend of the victim's ex-wife. He is accused of sending threatening e-mails under the pseudonym of "MYSALLY17" to the victim at his workplace. Liapis also allegedly mailed the victim photos of his house and car to prove he was watching him.

In many instances, those who are threatened by e-mail have little idea whether their Internet stalker will make good on a threat.

In Ms. Moubray's case, the warnings she received terrorized her so much that she had to take safety into her own hands. "I started carrying pepper spray, and I wouldn't go anywhere alone. My Dad bought me a gun," she says.

More often than not, police don't want to get involved in cases of Internet harassment until a physical crime occurs. Most cyberstalking laws, however, allow for prosecution if someone receives repeated e-mails threatening violence.

Even so, "the majority of police departments, district attorneys, and attorneys do not understand this, and the laws do not really protect you from this type of problem," says Mr. Hatcher.

Today, educating Internet users and lawmakers is the primary focus of groups like SafetyEd, WHOA and WiredPatrol. Each site has advice such as recommending use of a free e-mail account in chat rooms and a private address for friends.

Stalkers often stop once police or private agencies come to them with evidence that ties them to the threatening messages. In Moubray's case, the perpetrator lived in another state, so WHOA linked her up with a policeman in the stalker's hometown. One visit ended the Internet stalking.

"People can be very cool while they sit at their computer. Traditional stalkers have to be very angry to get close and threaten the victim, since there's a chance they will get punched in the nose," said Susan Catherine Herring, a fellow at Indiana University's Center for research on Learning & Technology.

Antistalking activists also say that for every case they take to police, scores more fail to meet the legal definition of cyberstalking. "One woman I know is getting 20,000 e-mails per day that say 'I love you'. . . but there's no threat, so it's not a crime," Hatcher says.

While many cyberstalkers fit the profile of loners with low-level jobs, the crime can be committed by anyone who lets an obsession take over part of his or her life. "You'd be surprised who does this; it's often doctors or lawyers," Hitchcock says. She adds that "only a handful" persist after being contacted by authorities.

For most victims, including Moubray, an end to the harassment is usually enough. "A big part of me is relieved; I will go places by myself now," she says. But, she adds, "I still carry my pepper spray."

8

Hackers

Cyber Alert

Arlene Weintraub and Jim Kerstetter

Cyber Alert: Portrait of an Ex-Hacker: A journey into the mind of KEVIN MITNICK shows just how vulnerable companies are to Internet crime.

It's April, and more than 1,600 corporate techies crowd into a ballroom in San Francisco's Moscone Center. The room buzzes with excitement as the star attraction, convicted computer hacker Kevin D. Mitnick, saunters onto the stage. He's on a panel of security gurus and legal experts ready to talk about whether companies should hire ex-hackers to safeguard their computer networks.

It's an explosive subject in the industry, and sparks fly as Mitnick takes on other panelists, including Ira Winkler, chief security strategist at Hewlett-Packard Co. After Winkler warns against hiring ex-hackers, Mitnick mocks him, claiming Winkler himself once hired ex-hackers to work at a consulting company he owned. "I know them personally," Mitnick says acidly. "I had traded [break-in secrets] with them."

The world's most notorious hacker is back in circulation. Known by his handle, "Condor," Mitnick spent 15 years marauding through the computers of the world's largest tech corporations, conning his victims into letting him into their systems. He served more than five years in jail. Only when his probation ended in January was he able to get back on the Internet and start a consulting company, Defensive Thinking LLC, which helps clients to prevent

---

"Cyber Alert" by Arlene Weintraub and Jim Kerstetter, *BusinessWeek,* June 9, 2003, p. 116. Reprinted by permission.

hackers from snagging credit-card numbers, medical records, and trade secrets.

His timing is impeccable. Hacking has reached epidemic proportions because of the explosive growth of the Internet. While Mitnick says he hacked for the sheer thrill of the break-in, never stealing money or destroying property, many of today's computer criminals have far more destructive goals in mind. The recent SQL Slammer "worm" shut down 13,000 Bank of America automated teller machines and slowed worldwide Internet traffic to a crawl. And intelligence experts fear terrorists could use the Net or other computer technology to attack the U.S. The Homeland Security Dept. is concerned that al Qaeda or another group could launch cyber and physical attacks simultaneously, attempting to disable safety systems at nuclear plants or air traffic control systems. "[The prospect of such an attack] is a tremendous threat," says Sallie McDonald, deputy chief of the information and warning division of Homeland Security.

Faced with such threats, companies and government agencies have been pouring cash into their defenses. The amount of money spent on computer security is expected to hit $13.5 billion this year, according to market researcher Forrester Research Inc., twice the total in 2000. The forecast for 2006: $20 billion.

Just spending money on the latest security software isn't enough, though. Corporations and governments are especially vulnerable if they ignore the human side of hacking. In security consultant parlance, it's called "social engineering"—and it's Mitnick's specialty. Hackers use it to dupe their victims into coughing up passwords and other sensitive information. In nearly all his attacks, Mitnick broke through the toughest network firewalls with persistence, a telephone, and a string of lies. His message to corporations: "There is no patch for stupidity." His own crimes show that the best key to any locked system is neither a computer nor a modem. It's a gullible human being. Mitnick once pulled a fast one on Motorola Inc. by posing as an employee and calling a Motorola engineer to persuade her to send him the core software for one of the company's new phones.

Mitnick's story is a journey inside the slippery mind of a hacker. It's *Catch Me If You Can* for the computer realm. A tour of Mitnick's psyche provides a clearer understanding of the dark forces that thrive in the digital world. His criminal career, say experts, is a point-by-point primer on what spawns hackers, how they think and operate, and how difficult it is for them to mend their ways. It's an alert to parents and educators to steer potential "Condors" in the right direction—before normal teenage rebellion turns into something poisonous. And it's a warning to government and corporate leaders to arm themselves against hackers and cyberterrorists.

These days, operating from the 17th floor of a fashionable West Los Angeles high-rise, the 39-year-old Mitnick strives to present himself as a reformed, mature tech consultant. His Defensive Thinking has attracted nine clients, whom he declines to identify. He has lined up more than 25 speaking gigs at seminars and private companies, each paying $5,000 to $20,000. And he has become something of a celebrity, publishing a book called *The Art of Deception* and making a cameo on television's *Alias* as a CIA agent.

Still, many corporations don't trust him. Not only is he a convicted con man but he's also world famous for it. "Do you hire the bank robber to guard your money? I don't think so," says Linda McCarthy, an executive security adviser at antivirus software maker Symantec Corp. The same fame that Mitnick relies on for marketing collides head-on with his credibility. Unless Mitnick can resolve this conflict, his consulting business may not thrive. And if his speaking engagements peter out once the novelty wears off, he might be tempted to fall back on his old ways. He denies it will happen. "I just won't fall back. It's not an option," he says.

Mitnick is out to prove to the world that he really has changed. He gave *BusinessWeek* access to his new life through a series of interviews and referrals to his family and friends. And he recounted the long, strange trip of his hacking career, the prison stints, the years on the run, and his attempts to come to terms with himself and society.

As an overweight, nerdy teen in Van Nuys, Calif., Mitnick was desperate for a place to belong and a way to succeed. The hacker's life gave him what he needed. He was the only child of Shelly Jaffe, a waitress who dragged him through four divorces and countless failed romances, mostly with men who gave little thought to keeping her bright but hyperactive son on the straight and narrow path. His father, Alan, a record promoter, was rarely around.

Left to his own devices, Mitnick escaped by learning magic. But card tricks soon bored him, so he sought out the hacker crowd in high school. Their high jinks—stealing computer passwords and cracking phone lines so they could make free calls—seemed like magic, but on a grander scale. "It was about the intrigue, the adventure, the pursuit of knowledge," says Mitnick. "I wanted to be in that clique." Recalls Ronen Rahaman, a friend of Mitnick's in high school: "Some guys wanted to do varsity football. Kevin wanted to do varsity hacking."

Mitnick was driven by the need to prove himself. Hackers are typically wallflowers, shunned by the in-crowd, so they look for ways to show off their smarts. "They show their power by screwing over the system," says Dr. Jerrold Post, director of the political psychology program at George Washington University. Mitnick shocked his friends with his audacity. At 16, he phoned a Digital Equipment Corp. system manager. Pretending to be the lead developer of a new DEC product, he snookered him into handing over a password. Once inside, he didn't steal anything. Breaking in was reward enough.

Computer crime can be addictive, and Mitnick knows it all too well. In his mid-20s, he hacked into DEC again, got arrested, and was convicted of felony computer fraud. He served a year in prison—including eight months in solitary confinement. Yet after his release, he couldn't resist the draw of the flickering computer screen, the challenge of that next great hack. "It's like being sober and having a guy show up at your place with a line of coke," Mitnick says. "He's enticing you. 'Come on ... it's just one time ... it won't hurt.'"

When the FBI started investigating his renewed hacking, he fled—leading to two wild years on the lam. As he ran from city to city, he took on phony identities and supported his hacking habit by working odd jobs—from systems administrator for a law firm to help desk analyst in Seattle. He was so convincing as Mr. Ordinary that his co-workers never suspected that after hours he was breaking into some of the best-protected computer systems in the world. He dodged the cops by monitoring police scanners to spy on the very people who were tracking him.

Even while on the run, Mitnick kept hacking obsessively. How wily was he? Shawn Nunley remembers Mitnick's incursions well. In February, 1994, Nunley was a systems administrator at software maker Novell Inc. Late one night, he got a phone call at home from Mitnick, who introduced himself as a Novell employee named Gabe Nault. He said he was on vacation and needed to connect to the network to work on a project. Having never met Nault, Nunley called Nault's voice mail to make sure the voice on it matched the one that had woken him in the middle of the night.

Mitnick was a step ahead of Nunley. The hacker had called a Novell network techie and convinced him to reset Nault's voice mail password. Then Mitnick left his own voice on the recording. "It seemed plausible. I gave him an account," says Nunley, now director of technology development at NetScaler Inc. in Santa Clara, Calif. Mitnick proceeded to steal a copy of the secret code for Novell's most important software product, NetWare. He just looked at the code, never using it for anything else.

Finally, though, Mitnick screwed up. On Christmas Eve, 1994, he hacked into the computer of Tsutomu Shimomura, a highly respected security expert at the San Diego Supercomputer Center. Bad move. Shimomura was incensed. He teamed up with the FBI and tracked Mitnick for two months, until they ran him to ground, surprising him in a Raleigh (N.C.) apartment, surrounded by telephone gear and fake driver's licenses.

It was during his second jail stay that Mitnick says he decided to mend his ways. He was denied access to anything his guards thought he might be able to use to hack from his cell—even a portable radio. "I was treated like Hannibal Lecter," he says. "It was absolutely the worst." So he channeled his energy into helping his lawyer fight his case. "Kevin's desire to hack came from a need to be successful at something," says his aunt, Chickie Leventhal, a bail bondswoman. "He just redirected that to his defense." He had been charged with 48 counts of computer, wire, and cell-phone fraud in 1995. By the time he pleaded guilty to seven of the charges in 1999, he had already served most of his five-year sentence.

Mitnick spent his probation trying to craft a normal, law-abiding life. He wrote the book. And even though he was not allowed to go on the Internet, he looked over other people's shoulders when they surfed the Net—like a modern-day Rip Van Winkle, fascinated with how much the cyberworld had changed during his long absence. He also has forged family bonds. He now lives in suburban Thousand Oaks, Calif., with his girlfriend, Darci Wood, and her 7-year-old daughter.

In his office in West Los Angeles, he's the picture of meticulous organization. He carries his BlackBerry handheld organizer wherever he goes, so he's sure to be on time for every appointment. "He's learning to channel his obsessiveness into something other than being obnoxious," says Don Wilson, a former boyfriend of Mitnick's mother and one of Mitnick's closest friends. "There's a sense of urgency to turn his life around."

The cops doubt that Mitnick is truly reformed, though. FBI agent Kenneth G. McGuire III, his relentless pursuer for years, worries that Mitnick is simply putting on an act—and that he won't be able to resist getting into trouble again. "He showed no remorse," says McGuire, whose office building is visible from the lobby of Mitnick's office. "He was laughing as he took the keys to the kingdom. He has no history to make him trustworthy."

Indeed, Mitnick is still furious at those who convicted him. When asked how people will be persuaded to trust him now, he launches into a fiery diatribe, raising his voice and slapping a conference room table in his office. He angrily denies prosecutors' assertions that he caused $5 million to $10 million in damage, and he insists he didn't deserve to be thrown in prison for five years. "The judge bought into the myth of Kevin Mitnick, as if I was the Osama bin Mitnick of the Internet," he says. "They wanted to create a cyber-bogeyman." He rages on for 40 minutes, listing all of the computer crimes ascribed to him that he didn't commit and attacking the government, the press, and the prison system for treating him unfairly.

Then he abruptly calms down, becomes sheepish. It's like the transformation of Mr. Hyde back into Dr. Jekyll. After he left prison and met some of his victims, he says, he realized the gravity of what he had done. He has apologized to several of them. "What I did was absolutely wrong. Unfortunately, I can't go back in time and fix it," he says. "There's nothing I can do but just live my life differently."

Mitnick acknowledges that it's a struggle to resist the urge to hack. One day, he says, he signed on to AOL Instant Messenger and was bombarded by greetings from teenage fans who had heard him reveal his screen name on a radio program. One, with the screen name Spikey 551, confessed that, at 14, he tried to hack into America Online and steal passwords. "I got caught in the first 10 minutes," Spikey lamented. Mitnick says he dashed out a quick reply. "Stay out of trouble," he advised. "You don't want to end up like me."

And corporations don't want to end up like Mitnick's victims. They are well advised to heed his warnings and plug the holes in their security systems caused by employees' gullibility. While he claims he has traded in his black hat for a white one, a whole new generation of con men is out there in cyber-space trying to one-up the master.

DON'T BE DUPED

For protection from social-engineering attacks, ex-hacker Kevin Mitnick suggests these precautions.

VERIFY THE CALL. If an employee you don't know calls asking for proprietary information or computer files, put the person on hold and call the extension to make sure the call is genuine.

ESTABLISH THE NEED TO KNOW. Don't send sensitive company info to anyone without checking with higher-ups to make sure the requester is authorized to have it.

BEWARE OF SURVEYS. Do not participate in phone surveys. Social engineers often call, posing as tech suppliers in need of data about their customers.

WATCH YOUR E-MAIL. Hackers use social engineering in e-mail, by using friendly subject lines and making it look as if the message is from someone you know. Do not click on links or delete files. You may be opening the door to a virus or a hacker.

BE SMART. Do not post sensitive info such as passwords in your work area. Deliverymen and other visitors may be hackers in disguise.

CATCH HIM IF YOU CAN: THE LIFE AND TIMES OF NOTORIOUS COMPUTER HACKER KEVIN MITNICK

AUG. 6, 1963. Kevin David Mitnick is born in Van Nuys, Calif., to Shelly Jaffe, a waitress, and Alan Mitnick, a record promoter. They divorce two years later.

1981. Mitnick is arrested for the first time, for hacking into Pacific Bell's computers.

1987. Mitnick is arrested again—this time for hacking into Santa Cruz Operation, a software company.

1989. Mitnick serves one year in prison—including eight months in solitary confinement—for hacking into Digital Equipment Corp. Toward the end of his three years on probation, he lapses back into hacking. He flees a warrant issued for his arrest and becomes a fugitive.

FEB. 15, 1995. The FBI tracks Mitnick down in Raleigh, N.C., and arrests him.

MAR. 16, 1999. He pleads guilty to seven counts of wire and computer fraud.

JAN. 21, 2000. Mitnick is released from prison eight months early, but he's required to stay clear of the Net during his three-year probation.

JAN. 21, 2003. Mitnick logs on to the Net for the first time in eight years—and launches a career as a security consultant.

9

The Scope of the Problem

Big Bad World

Stephen Marlin

Actually, when it comes to computer security, it's a small—and threatening—world. A global reach calls for global security measures.

No computer connected to a network is completely safe. Any computer that communicates with another, even occasionally, can fall victim to the threats that race around our interconnected world. Hackers live in any country. And the worms and viruses with the cute names—Code Red, Blaster, Nimba, Slammer, Sobig—don't recognize national borders. "There's no difference between the Blaster that hits Europe or the United States," says Gene Fredriksen, VP of information security at financial-services firm Raymond James & Associates, which has offices in several foreign countries. "We all swim in the same pool."

Cultures may differ and languages may vary, but the security threats IT systems around the world face are pretty much the same, according to the InformationWeek 2003 Global Information Security Survey of 2,500 business-technology and security professionals. And the tactics used to fend off those threats are similar the world over.

First the good news. In the 12 months ending in July, virus, worm, and Trojan-horse attacks hit 45% of sites surveyed, down dramatically from 66% in the same period two years ago. Those kinds of attacks occurred more often in South America (55%) and the Asia-Pacific region (49%) than in North America (46%) and Europe (41%). About 15% of sites surveyed suffered denial-of-service attacks, the same as in 2001, but more businesses in Asia-Pacific (19%) and North America (19%) experienced such attacks than companies in South America (14%) or Europe (11%).

As businesses are repeatedly hit by viruses, worms, and denial-of-service attacks that travel over the Internet, it's no surprise that security managers are paying more attention to external threats. Of the 1,255 sites reporting security breaches this year, 58% point the finger at hackers or terrorists (up from 42% in 2000) and 32% cite unauthorized users or employees (up from 22% in 2000). The number of survey respondents who suspect current or former employees declined slightly.

There are regional differences. Businesses in South America and the Asia-Pacific region, which have been getting hit harder by worms and viruses, plan to increase their security spending more than other regions. Some 53% of South American companies and 44% of Asia-Pacific companies say they'll boost their security spending, compared with 39% in North America and 30% in Europe. Only about 10% of companies in all regions say they'll spend less on security.

Most South American (71%), North American (68%), and Asia-Pacific (64%) businesses plan to improve operating-system security. Another top business priority is enhancing application security: South America, 74%; Asia-Pacific, 68%; North America, 63%. The main problem for many businesses is simply keeping up with the number of threats, the speed with which they attack, and the number of patches they must test and deploy to protect their systems. The Blaster worm first struck on Aug. 11 and within a week infected more than 1.4 million systems worldwide, even though a patch was available to protect systems. Clearly, many people—mostly home users, but many businesses and government entities around the world—hadn't bothered to install the patch; those who had installed it helped keep disruption to a minimum.

ABN Amro, an international bank with 3,000 branches in more than 60 countries, understands the importance of keeping security up to date. Following the Nimba and Slammer attacks, "we identified impacts on revenues in the tens of millions of dollars, mostly because of trading systems that went down," says Craig Hollenbaugh, head of standards and controls in the bank's wholesale division.

ABN Amro relies on a technology unit in the United Kingdom to analyze security threats and determine how urgent it is to install patches. Based on the unit's evaluation that Blaster posed a high-risk threat, the bank moved aggressively to patch systems. "We threw everybody at it and performed integration testing to make sure the mission-critical applications worked with the patch," Hollenbaugh says. "We fared well with this one."

Even when the threat is clearly understood and a patch is available, security managers can face resistance. At Prudential Financial Services Inc., which has offices in more than 25 countries, some business units didn't want to take the time to install software fixes. "They were questioning why we were putting them through this patching misery," says Ken Tyminski, chief information security officer. "They had to bring in developers who had to work late, and other projects had to be put on the side."

The cost of being secure can be daunting: Between 200 and 300 application developers did tests to make sure the patch wouldn't hurt Prudential's most-important applications, and more than 150 people spent several days installing the patch throughout the company's IT infrastructure.

Those efforts, combined with tighter security policies, ongoing security-awareness training, and properly placed defensive technology, all worked together to keep Blaster at bay. To improve security even more, Prudential is completing a rollout of 20,000 copies of Sygate Secure Enterprise, which provides desktop firewall and system-security policy enforcement, to remote and mobile employees. That should help the company enforce security polices, as well as increase control over and reduce the cost of managing remote systems, which often provide the hole through which viruses and worms enter company networks. "It was a good feeling knowing it was out there," Tyminski says. "We had another layer of protection in our defenses." Just like Prudential, about half of all survey respondents say they'll be securing remote users. BT Group plc (formerly British Telecom) is installing personal firewalls from security vendor InfoExpress for 5,000 remote and mobile workers. Currently, BT employees are forbidden from logging on to the Internet or untrusted networks with their notebooks. "This is part of an integrated approach to desktop security," says Paul Washington, a manager and operational team leader with BT Exact, the research, technology, and operations arm of BT Group. "You need the virtual private network, the personal firewall, and the antivirus—all three things—to make a secure desktop."

Another crucial step for multinational companies is to impose standards and policies worldwide. APL Ltd., a subsidiary of Neptune Orient Lines, has a fleet of 80 container ships that serves more than 100 markets around the world. The $3.4 billion-a-year shipper is moving more applications to the Web and exploring products to help defend against Web-based attacks, which analysts say make up about 80% of all hacker attacks.

"We have to do everything on a global basis so there's no isolation on a regional basis," says David Arbo, director of information security. He's looking at an integrated offering that combines a Web-security application gateway from NetContinuum Inc. and application security-assessment software from SPI Dynamics Inc. APL intends to set up a security console to give it a complete picture of security throughout its global operations. "Manually, you can't keep up," Arbo says. "We're stretched to serve so many areas, and we have so many desktops, for us not to have a tool like that."

The company also is looking to improve the physical security of its shipping ports and IT systems. APL uses radio-frequency identification technology for building access, and it's examining smart cards and tokens with RFID-type technology. "We're looking for some sort of token that would serve a dual role for physical and logical [IT] access," he says. Like APL, many companies want to integrate physical and computer security. Some 35% of those surveyed called it a strategic priority, up from 27% in 2002.

Few, however, have as great a need as the U.S. Department of Defense. The agency has launched an initiative called Common Access Card, which features a smart card enabled with public-key-infrastructure capabilities that runs the Java Card run-time environment on chips with 32 Kbytes of memory. The department has issued more than 3 million cards to military personnel and contractors. They are used to gain access to military bases around the world, log on to computers, obtain medical or other benefits, and digitally sign and encrypt E-mail. The military is issuing 10,000 cards a day at about 1,500 locations in 15 countries and hopes to have 4.3 million cards deployed by the end of the year. More than 150,000 smart-card readers also have been deployed.

"We've always said that we're trying to bring the Department of Defense to the same place that the credit-card world has always been," says Bill Boggess, a division chief for the access- and authentication-technology division at the Defense Manpower Data Center. "Today, you can't buy at McDonald's without them prechecking your card." The department hopes its card will provide that type of swift authorization for its personnel around the world. In addition to protecting against enemy threats, just keeping track of the large number of people entering and exiting military facilities poses a challenge. One base in the Midwest has 400,000 personnel coming and going each day, Boggess notes. "When you're dealing with numbers like 4.4 million active duty and reservists, knowing who they are and where they are when they log on to systems is a huge step forward," he says.

Deploying up-to-date security in the military, where orders are usually followed, may be easier than in the private sector. Users often become complacent when they read about serious worms and viruses and then see little disruption to their companies' IT systems. A security analyst at a major software maker, who asked not to be identified, saw a lot of resistance in the past month. "Some of our business units didn't want to patch. Some pushed back, saying it would postpone other priorities. Some just ignored our call to patch," he says. "Those units were the first to look like the Fourth of July when the worm got into our networks."

More automated patching tools could help managers overcome that resistance. "We're looking at ways to push the patch out," says the software-company security analyst. "Next time, we'll have the resources to deploy the patch and the corporate policies to make sure each unit does its part to protect our systems."

Making sure employees understand that security is everyone's responsibility is key, and there's much work that still needs to be done to accomplish that. Yes, deploying sound security technologies is necessary to secure global IT systems. But just as important is enforcing companywide security policies and raising the security awareness of all employees, Prudential's Tyminski says.

A virus, worm, hacker, or insider-gone-bad can strike at any time, and computer users need to understand that every connected computer—and the person using it—is on the front line of the battle. Raising security awareness at Prudential is one of Tyminski's most-important accomplishments during his three years on the job, he says. "When I used to ask who was responsible for security at Prudential, everyone used to say me," he says. "Now when I ask, most everyone raises their hands, because they now know they each play their own important roles."

10

Juvenile Cyber Crime

Enlisting the Young as White-Hat Hackers

Julie Flaherty

O N a Wednesday evening, in an office suite appointed with Pentium II's and little else, 10 teenagers were doing Andrew Robinson's bidding. Fortified by pizza and soda, they studied a computer system's weaknesses, looking for ways to break in and steal information. Mr. Robinson urged them on, like a modern-day Fagin goading his band of pickpockets.

Mr. Robinson, 38, who runs a small information security company in nearby Portland, had less-than-nefarious plans in mind, however. His free after-school program is intended to teach teenagers the basics of ethical hacking, or protecting a company's computer system from attack by learning how to attack it yourself.

The program, called Tiger Team, named for the professional consultants who analyze system security risk, teaches young hackers to use their skills for good instead of evil. Working as two teams, the teenagers play a virtual game of capture the flag, trying to crack the other team's network and do damage while defending their own. An honor code keeps them from creating mischief outside their labs.

Mr. Robinson got the idea for this "information security sandbox" three years ago at a job fair, where he met a teenager who had been arrested for low-level hacking. Mr. Robinson saw his setbacks as a waste, considering the constant demand for information security professionals. So he created a non-profit organization, the Internet Security Foundation, dedicated to educating the public about information security. Its pilot project, Tiger Team, began last month.

"Here's how you can do this legally, within a moral and ethical framework, and make a good amount of money doing it," Mr. Robinson said. "It fills the need of the companies, and more and more since 9/11, it fills the need of the country for cybersecurity."

It could also fill a need for the state of Maine, which loses many of its skilled young people to jobs in other states. Mr. Robinson estimated that someone with five years of experience in information security could command a salary of $70,000 to $90,000 here.

"That's in the top 1 percent of wage earners in the state," he said. "For at least a few hundred kids, perhaps we can provide an alternative to leaving. They can do this from their homes, and a lot of people do."

Finding participants was easy. About 50 teenagers from southern Maine contacted Mr. Robinson after reading about his idea in the local newspapers. More than a third said they had done something that could be construed as hacking.

"There were a couple who refused to answer the question about whether they had been in trouble for it," Mr. Robinson said. "I think most of that was just bravado."

He doubts he will convert anyone truly attracted to hacking's antisocial side. "Somebody who was sort of the Elite Hackzor, or whatever you want to call it, would probably not have applied for this program." he said. "If they were already in the dark side, they would probably not come here."

The teenagers, boys who average about 16 years in age, do wield some power. All were required to have experience configuring different kinds of operating systems, including a Mac or Unix-based one, and writing computer programs.

"They weren't script kiddies," Mr. Robinson said, referring to system crackers who wage attacks with programs written by savvier coders, often without understanding them. "They have all the skills that they need to cause trouble, and some of them may have even started doing some of those things just for fun."

The most serious breaches the applicants confessed to were outwitting a Web site's access controls to view content that they shouldn't have. "You can use your imagination for what that might be for, in this case, all teenage boys," Mr. Robinson said.

In the second week of the seven-week program, the students sat patiently through two presentations on the business side of information security, from creating a risk assessment to securing management support. But the third speaker had trouble getting through his talk on finding a system's weaknesses because the students interrupted with questions.

"We put the interesting things last," said Justin Smith, 27, a Tiger Team volunteer and a network analyst in Mr. Robinson's company, NMI

InfoSecurity Solutions. Mr. Smith said the students had performed so well that the instructors had to accelerate the instruction.

"I kept saying that we were going to have a hard time staying ahead of these guys," he said. (Indeed, they were bright enough to cajole Mr. Robinson into ordering them pizza.)

Between lectures, the two teams zipped off to their separate lab rooms, where competition was already building.

"There's been a little bit of window spying," said Tristan Fisher, 18.

Perhaps some shifty scouting technique employing Microsoft Windows? Not quite.

"We're on the first floor," Mr. Fisher said, pulling aside the blinds to reveal the parking lot. "Every now and then we'll see someone walk over to our window and peek in."

An unclosed lab door is also fair game. Mr. Robinson, who is careful to turn all important paperwork on his desk face down before receiving visitors, teaches students that not all hacking is done electronically.

Scott Anderson, 18, a high school senior, is giving serious thought to going into the information security profession. "This is probably the only link I have to getting a job when I graduate," he said, adding that he had barely passing grades.

Good grades are not a requirement for the program. Mr. Robinson, who related that he himself had excellent standardized test scores but poor grades, said he empathized with students who say they are bored with school. It was not until an uncle who taught computer science at the University of Maine got him into some college-level classes, he said, that he saw his own future open up.

Bill Seretta thought the program was just right for his son Will, a 10th-grader with computer inclinations and "grades all over the map."

"If he didn't have to go to school he wouldn't," Mr. Seretta said. "The structure doesn't interest him."

Although all the participants count computing as a hobby, Mr. Seretta considers the format—hands on, fast-paced—more important than the subject. "This is about learning and not technology," he said.

The office space, the computers and the Internet connection have all been donated, mostly by banks and other organizations that recognize the need for information security. But Mr. Robinson met with some initial qualms.

"Some of them grilled us pretty heavily on the concept of, 'Well, aren't you training hackers?'" he said. "I go, yeah. I have a black belt in martial arts. If I wanted to be a bad guy, I could go and hurt people. But I don't do it. That's not the emphasis of the program."

The students are getting a good dose of ethics along with some sobering words about legal repercussions. Scheduled guest speakers include a lawyer and a police officer, and Mr. Robinson is hoping to recruit a speaker from the Federal Bureau of Investigation.

"Yes, we are teaching them to be hackers," he said, "but wouldn't you rather have them on your side?"

12

Online Gambling Needs Regulation

Economy, Consumer Safety Will Benefit from Changes to Outdated Law

WASHINGTON, Sept. 17/PRNewswire/—Experts met in Washington yesterday to discuss Internet gambling, and ways to regulate it. Hosted by BETonSPORTS plc, the world's largest on-line wagering service, the summit was part of a national public policy initiative called "Proposition 1: To Regulate or Prohibit Online Gambling." Designed to create a framework for lawmakers to regulate the industry, today's summit was the second in a series of meetings to be held across the U.S. this month.

Today's discussion brought together experts in law, academia, industry, advertising and media, to debate whether online gaming should be legal in the United States. The issues surrounding regulation versus prohibition of the online gaming industry were addressed, with an emphasis on the need to develop federal regulation that will both recognize the growth and popularity of online gambling and provide key consumer protections. The panel's overall consensus was that online gaming could operate legally and safely in the United States, provided that the federal government establishes regulations to protect consumers.

"Economy, Consumer Safety Will Benefit from Changes to Outdated Law,"
PR Newswire, Sept. 17, 2004. Reprinted by permission.

Keith Whyte, executive director of the National Council on Problem Gambling, explained that consumer protection safeguards should apply to all gambling, including land-based and Internet gaming.

"The distinctions between the types of gambling, based on how they're delivered to the participant, seem arbitrary," he explained. "The point is, the operator has the obligation to develop responsible gaming policies, regardless of whether the gambling is on the lottery, at a church bingo night, or on the Internet. There seems to be no theoretical reason that Internet gambling operators could not develop programs that meet or exceed current land-based responsible gaming practices."

Agreeing with Whytes' assessment, David Carruthers, CEO of BETonSPORTS plc added, "We have to act responsibly. We want to set the example for hosting a safe Internet site, and we're willing to do whatever it takes. BETonSPORTS is offering itself as a rallying force for sensible regulation."

During the discussion, Carruthers explained that sensible regulation on gambling is right for the consumer, the operator, and the government. For the consumer, because it assures that operators are conducting business at a legitimate caliber and assures that consumers' money is secure; the operator, because it allows them to carry out their business in a secure, stable and predictable environment; and the government, because it allows them the opportunity to capitalize on revenues upwards of $100 billion (the amount Americans bet on sports every year) and will produce additional jobs in the U.S.

The legalization of Internet gaming would not only contribute additional jobs and taxation dollars to the U.S. economy, it would also clarify the law on Internet gaming advertising with U.S.-based companies; this would in turn generate even more money for the economy. William Heberer, an attorney with the firm of Manatt, Phelps and Philips LLP, expanded upon the issue of advertising and referred to the 1961 Wire Communications Act—the law that the Department of Justice claims makes wagering over the Internet illegal.

"The Wire Act is an antiquated statute that the government is using to intimidate companies from accepting advertising for Internet gambling sites," Heberer stated. "This is a law that was developed to stop racketeering over the phone more than 50 years ago. They are manipulating the law to cover a technology that was not even invented when the Act was written."

Added Emily Hancock, an attorney with Steptoe & Johnson LLP, "The DOJ's actions are not only overreaching but if this leads to outright prohibition it will put an unreasonable burden on the Internet service providers to block online gambling."

Heberer also criticized outright prohibition no more effective than "the little boy with his finger in the dyke. There will be no way to enforce it with consumers. From a consumer point of view it's better for government to bring online gambling into the light of day."

"This is the time to address Internet gaming regulation," Carruthers concluded. "I come from a culture where I have seen regulation work, and the United States has a right to see for themselves."

The Summit tour will continue into Chicago on September 22 and Los Angeles on September 24.

Also part of the initiative is a series of college campus debates and an advertising campaign.

COLLEGE DEBATES

BETonSPORTS will host a series of debates that tackle the issues surrounding the growth and proliferation of online gambling on college campuses—from whether "responsible gambling" is a contradiction in terms, to exploration of the ethical issues of student-athletes wagering on collegiate games.

Students make up a growing part of the online gambling market and yet they have not been actively engaged on the issues, let alone discussion on what constitutes responsible online gambling. Moreover, according to the NCAA, gambling by student-athletes is occurring at a "startling" rate. As students continue to use the Internet for gambling, these debates will help them become better informed on the issues, understand responsible gambling, and have an impact on public policy-making.

NATIONAL ADVERTISING CAMPAIGN

As part of BETonSPORTS' "Right to Wager" campaign, television advertisements making the case for online gambling enthusiasts' right to decide whether to wager online or not have started airing in 20 cities across the U.S. including Chicago, Los Angeles, New York and Washington, D.C. The television ads are running in conjunction with an online campaign where visitors are asked to sign a petition and/or send a letter to their congressman. Print advertising is set to run in newspapers nationwide as well.

For a complete list of Summit panel members, to obtain a copy of the advertisements, or to participate in or attend either the Summit meetings or the College Debates, please contact Kajal Jhaveri, Ruder Finn, at 212-593-5864 or jhaverik@ruderfinn.com.

ABOUT BETonSPORTS PLC

BETonSPORTS, which operates the largest online wagering service in the world, is committed to providing its clients with the most value for their wagering dollar and quality customer service capabilities. Headquartered in San JosA[c], Costa Rica, the company is licensed in the Caribbean, Central America and Europe, and has obtained a bookmakers permit in the UK, where gambling has been a legal and respected tradition for over forty years. The company trades under the symbol BSS.L on the London Stock Exchange's Alterative Investment Market. BETonSPORTS.com has been ranked the number one sportsbook by a number of leading industry organizations, including the Offshore Gaming Association (OSGA), the International Sports Book Council (ISBC) and Insiders Football Guide. Visit http://www.betonsports. com/ for more information.

Not content with one arrest, the Tiptons continued posing online as teenage girls. And they've become pretty good at it.

"None of the cases has gone to trial because it's so tight," says Bulleit, who notes that the Tiptons document all their correspondence with the men. "I'm sure their defense lawyers look at what we've got and tell them to forget it."

Since Evans' arrest, the Tiptons have helped police nab two other sex offenders, Keith Morgan Bishop, a truck driver from Arkansas, and Ludwig Velarde Ruiz, a Virginia paralegal whom Maitland police arrested in January when he arrived to meet a 12-year-old but discovered a cop with handcuffs instead.

Like Evans, Bishop pleaded guilty. Police in Virginia found so much child pornography on Ruiz's computer that they planned to charge him with 35 counts of child pornography as well as with soliciting sex with a minor.

Together, the charges could have sent him to jail for years. Ruiz skipped bail, and police think he has fled the country. Bishop, meanwhile, served six months in jail and is now a registered sex offender.

The police and those who know Kenny Tipton say he's the primary reason for the arrests.

"He's not one to toot his own horn," says Maitland attorney Paul West, who helped Tipton file incorporation papers for his fledgling nonprofit organization, Keeping Internet Kids Safe. "He just has a passion for keeping the predators away from kids."

Ironically, Kenny and Sharon Tipton met online. Kenny, divorced from his first wife, was visiting chat rooms when he first came across Sharon, who lived in Maryland. After eight months of correspondence, they finally met in 2001 when Kenny bought Sharon a plane ticket to visit him in Florida. They married the next year.

Nowadays, the Tiptons are still watching for online predators, but Kenny is also busy chasing down spammers who send porn-related e-mails to unsuspecting people. "It's not rocket science," he says. "There's always a trail."

But fighting porn spammers has made him a target. Spammers have broken into his AOL account, hacked into his Keeping Internet Kids Safe Web site, and threatened to sue him. One even threatened to kill him.

"Whether they'll ever show up at my door, I don't know," he says. "But these guys said they would break into my account, and they did." So Tipton plays it safe. He and his family live in a gated apartment community outside Orlando. He avoids giving out his daughter's age or first name. And he refuses to buy anything online.

For Kenny and Sharon Tipton, the battle continues in what may prove to be a very long war. He's currently flooding AOL with letters, urging the company to better monitor its chat rooms and scour them of porn spam. He also speaks to community groups about his crusade.

"I remember one lady saying, 'You're not going to stop all that on the Internet. You can't make a difference,'" Kenny says. "The truth is, we have, and we can."

14

Fighting Cyber Crime

The Code Warriors

Erick Roston with David Aucsmith, Dan Geer, Charles Palmer, Sal Stolfo, and Michael Vatis

The Code Warriors: Technologists are deputies in the fight against terrorism. How are they protecting us—and what must you do on your own? (TIME Bonus Section December 2003: Inside Business/Security)

Cantor Fitzgerald, the financial-services firm that occupied the top floors of a World Trade Center tower, has more real-world experience with computers and terrorism than any other company. It lost more than 700 of its 1,000 New York City employees on Sept. 11. Despite obstacles that were unforeseeable in any emergency contingency plan and that challenged the limits of emotional endurance, survivors managed to reopen with the bond markets 47 hours later.

How did they do it? Within three hours of the attack, technology employees made it to a seven-month-old backup facility across the Hudson River in Roselle Park, N.J., and contacted the London office. Reassigning tasks on the fly between London and Roselle Park, they brought processing and storage systems online, installed truckloads of new equipment with help from Microsoft and Cisco Systems, and in isolated cases even reconstituted passwords of fallen colleagues, who—like me and probably you—made them personal and easily remembered.

Behind the superlative heroism of this tale lie the two key mandates of the new century: prevent physical attacks and make computers safe from intruders. As the nation girds against mortal threats, many experts fear we will overlook the danger to our information, wealth and identities, all now reduced to 0s and 1s spinning through silicon. The more we rely on computers, the more vulnerable we are to attack or failure.

How ready are businesses and governments for what onlookers more than 10 years ago began calling a "digital Pearl Harbor"? Physical attacks are targeted to specific geographic areas; if you're not there, you're probably safe. But if you have computers or are affected by them—and that's everybody—you're at risk of inconvenience, intrusion or, technologists fear, much worse. Building better defenses to protect home computers, business networks and civic infrastructure must therefore be—however cliched it is to say—the Next Big Thing. In 1999 security incidents reported to the CERT Command Center, a federally funded research group, totaled 9,859; from January to September of this year, there were 114,855. Security spending has grown 28% a year since 2001, the Gartner research firm reports, while overall tech budgets have expanded just 6%. And a three-day war game in July 2002 run by Gartner and the U.S. Naval War College tentatively answered the Pearl Harbor question. It is possible, they concluded, that without proper cybersecurity—both tools and behavior—highly skilled hackers could disrupt the nation's electrical, financial and telecommunications systems.

In a year in which viruses and worms made the front page and identity theft reached an all-time high, TIME's Board of Technologists keyed us into current cyberthreats and offered us its best solutions. On hand for our round table were David Aucsmith, architect and chief technology officer of Microsoft's Security Business Unit; Dan Geer, a consultant, entrepreneur and lead author of a recent report on the potential risk that widespread use of Microsoft products places on security; Charles Palmer, director of IBM Security & Privacy Research; Sal Stolfo, a Columbia University computer-science professor and member of Professionals for Cyber Defense; and Michael Vatis, an attorney with Fried, Frank, Harris, Shriver & Jacobson and director of the FBI's National Infrastructure Protection Center from 1998 to 2001.

SECURITY 101

"I always say, 'As far as we know,' no one has written a virus or worm that can bring down all the communications. But that opening disclaimer is very important."
—*Charles Palmer*

Sept. 11 taught us that the spectrum of potential threats is as wide as the imagination. The same could be said for vulnerabilities to the computers we depend on. Families must guard their computers against novice vandals planting viruses or against more advanced intruders leeching your computing power to launch a cyberattack on someone else. Despite the spate of devastating viruses this year—Slammer in January, Blaster and Sobig in August—the threat has evolved past the 17-year-old hacker, past the lone thief who steals and reveals credit-card data. Businesses must now watch for organized-crime groups adept at lifting valuable, private information and extorting money with it. The Federal Government and key industries must keep aspiring cyberterrorists from busting open dams or shorting out our electric grid from a keyboard in Pakistan. Reason: al-Qaeda and other terrorist groups have started scoping infrastructure and learning about cyberattack techniques.

The main reason for our vulnerability is that scientists created the Internet as an open network to share information; they never anticipated its dark side. Now, having unleashed it, they must retroactively make it closed and safe from these threats. "Value has moved into cyberspace," Aucsmith said, "and there are real criminals moving there as well." He noted that Willie Sutton, the legendary bank robber, said he cracked safes "because that's where the money is."

THE HUMAN THREAT

"If you can fault our industry—we realized a little bit too late that we did indeed connect everybody, including the bad guys." —David Aucsmith

Humans strike at computer systems in one of two ways, through malevolence or incompetence. Unfortunately for law-enforcement agencies and the people they protect, the bad guys are getting much better at what they do.

The FBI in the past two years has reinforced its cybercrime division as mercenaries in the global capitals of hackerdom—Russia, Brazil, the Philippines—team up with traditional organized-crime groups to infiltrate ATM systems or hold corporate databases hostage. Before he became mayor of New York City, Michael Bloomberg helped the FBI and Scotland Yard foil a plot by a Kazakh national who was threatening to break into the computers of Bloomberg's financial-information company unless he was paid off. In November 2000 the FBI busted two Russians who had been trying to extort money from an American Internet company—undercover agents had lured them to the U.S. with compliments and a fake job offer. And the FBI, burned in 2001 by the Robert Hanssen spy scandal, knows as well as anyone else the danger caused by internal security threats, which nationwide are growing even faster than external ones.

Incompetence can be just as wily an opponent. Before the desktop revolution, the average computer user had to know much more about how computers work than he or she does today. Now we don't need to know much but still foul up what we should know, like not opening attachments to unsolicited e-mail. Consumers also repeatedly fail to install security available to them. Manufacturers regularly issue programs called patches that fix newly found flaws in software. Microsoft gives consumers several options for patch delivery, from automatic downloads to manual installation. Free security upgrades: What could be easier?

Virus writers take advantage of the gap between the time a patch is issued to cover a newly discovered flaw and the time users actually download the patch. In that window, they are able to study the flaw, write their destructive virus and let it loose. And they have been getting better at it—so much better, in fact, that Microsoft last month introduced a stricter security regimen. The company will release its patches monthly to make life more predictable for corporate and individual customers. At the end of October, Bill Gates previewed the firm's Longhorn operating system (due in 2006), emphasizing its security advances.

Companies are trying to automate security so that customers needn't worry about it: today's software is in many cases so overgrown and bloated that the complexity overwhelms programmers. The number of flaws increases geometrically with the volume of code. "Complexity is the enemy of security," Palmer said.

The software industry is learning from the credit-card industry, which has digitized crime watching based on card users' behavior. Basically, the credit-card companies monitor your card patterns, and when something out of the ordinary happens—a card is used overseas, yet the cardholder rarely travels, for example—the alarm goes off. Is the cardholder really in London? It sounds creepy and intrusive, but tracking exceptions to detect intruders is the basis for several new security approaches. And it has already become an invisible part of our lives. Stolfo has a start-up called System Detection, a two-year-old company whose tools scan networks and applications for code that shouldn't be there. Surveillance of this variety is effective—and it is going to be more pervasive. A number of start-ups are developing technology that sniffs out "aberrant" behavior. Like it or not, somebody is going to be watching.

MARKET SPEED

"I don't personally want to bash any individual company or manufacturer. I would rather bash them all." —Sal Stolfo

Suppose 90% of the world's automobiles used the same engine, and an undetected flaw suddenly emerged that shut them all down. We're talking global gridlock.

That's the worst nightmare for Microsoft, the company that provides 90% of the world's desktop operating systems and a similar proportion of its Internet browsers. Microsoft earned its market share, but with that dominance comes the vulnerability of what computer geeks call monoculture. The near monopoly undermines security by making everyone's computers susceptible to the same flaws (you need only note the $2 billion in losses caused by the Sobig worm to understand). Critics point to parallels in the natural world to explain what happens when life becomes too dependent on a single source. "The Irish potato famine killed a country. The boll weevil killed an economy," Geer said.

"It is self-evident that the desktops of the world are clones ripe for the slaughter"—unless they are Macs or run the open-source Linux software, both underdogs that hackers are less likely to subvert. The latter's ability to be guarded and upgraded on the fly by a universe of programmers offers some protection against the megaviruses. Linux's tamper resistance is one reason governments in particular are showing great interest in Linux-based operating systems.

Unfortunately, most business customers don't know how to determine their own security risk. "They just wing it, largely," Vatis said. Companies such as AIG and Chubb offer cyberinsurance, but the industry lacks the actuarial data it has for traditional lines. Large companies can't just redesign products with more deeply embedded security features, because customers don't take well to mandates to completely trash their old systems for new ones. "It would be considerably easier if I were allowed to start from the ground, build a secure system and deploy," said Aucsmith. Until that happens, the data we entrust to companies might be guarded by the cyberequivalent of a dozing senior citizen with a fake cop badge.

CYBERNATIONAL SECURITY

"As long as the state of security remains where it is today, the government will never have attack-response capabilities. We will remain too much of a target-rich environment." —Michael Vatis

Put more bluntly, our country's critical data systems are the World Trade towers, and the hijacked planes are heading in their direction. Criminals have discovered how much easier it is to rob banks with a keyboard than a mask and gun. Will terrorists figure out how to shut down the banking system and strangle the economy? Information technology controls the nation's physical infrastructure—nuclear plants, air-traffic control, water systems—like a central nervous system. "Hits against the IT network will cascade to the other critical infrastructures," Stolfo said. (Consider the cascading effect of this year's blackout.)

A 2002 National Academy of Sciences report stated that our willingness and ability to deal with threats relative to their magnitude had grown worse since the organization's first report in 1991. "Nobody owns the problem," Stolfo said. Professionals for Cyber Defense, Stolfo's group, and Vatis have independently called for a Manhattan Project for security that would take responsibility for safeguarding these critical networks.

That's an awesome task, and it won't be completed overnight. "These threats are not new," asserts Robert Liscouski, Assistant Secretary of Homeland Security, who is shuffling several far-flung federal agencies into one National Cyber Security Division (NCSD). He says "digital Pearl Harbor" scenarios are exaggerated: "That's a bit of an overplay for me, and I get paid to worry about this stuff." In October, Amit Yoran, a former vice president of the Internet security firm Symantec, became head of the NCSD, which will attempt to seek and destroy vulnerabilities in cyberspace, issue warnings in real time and foster communication with the vast private sector, which owns 85% of the infrastructure.

The Federal Government is nipping at the problem elsewhere. Hard-core technophiles get queasy at the notion of Congress creating laws that tell them how to do their arcane jobs. Yet three of the most significant laws of the past 10 years—the Health Insurance Portability and Accountability Act (1996), the Gramm-Leach-Bliley financial-modernization law (1999) and last year's Sarbanes-Oxley corporate-reform act—all have mandates to protect and secure data. Still needed, Geer argued, are laws that hold companies liable for holes in their security that make us vulnerable to attacks from elsewhere. Responsibility for passive negligence "might be better than, God help us, the U.S. Senate imposing an argument about what the limits of liability should be," he said.

Generals, the saying goes, are always fighting the last war. With the nation understandably focused on aviation security and biological, nuclear and chemical threats, technologists hope their message—that network vulnerabilities are real and that a significant failure could muck up everything else—is getting through. Security risk is a shifting balance between individual and institutional responsibilities and vigilance. Or, as Geer succinctly put it, "The price of freedom is the probability of crime."

"Headlines screaming DOOM! may be as right as they are disingenuous." —Dan Geer

"No lay user would say that security technology today is easy to use." —Michael Vatis

15

Jurisdictional Challenges

Internet Crime Becomes More International Phenomenon

Dana Ambrosini

Apr. 28—NORWALK, Conn.—Cybercrime isn't just an activity for mischievous, computer-savvy youth.

Expert "crackers," or computer hackers involved in cybercrime, have set up companies, sometimes with legitimate business fronts, for the sole purpose of illegally breaking into other companies' computers for financial gain, said Joe Dooley, a special agent with the Federal Bureau of Investigation.

Eastern Europe, the former Soviet Union and Asia are hotbeds of such activity, Dooley told an audience of about 50 business representatives at a SACIA conference on cybercrime Friday. SACIA is the business council of southwestern Connecticut.

Connecticut, being the wealthiest state in the nation, and a big location for financial transaction companies, is a prime target, Dooley said.

Crackers are involved in any number of Internet schemes involving everything from fraud operations to identity theft to extortion, Dooley said.

"The Internet is simply a new venue for the same crimes we've seen before," Dooley said.

Not using your credit card online won't protect you either, Dooley said. "Folks are afraid of using cards online," he said. "You should be afraid every time you use your credit card."

That's because hackers are breaking into the databases of retailers and taking entire lists of credit card numbers, Dooley said.

One particularly egregious offender was accused, among numerous other cybercrimes, of extorting money out of companies he'd broken into with threats that he would expose or destroy their information.

U.S. law enforcement officers lured the suspect, Alexey Ivanov, from Russia to the United States, where he is now being held in prison while awaiting trial, said Mark Califano, assistant U.S. attorney.

Other hackers steal source codes and software products so they can put them out for free downloads on the Internet.

It may seem egalitarian, but "freeing" source code that other individuals have slaved to create is devastating to smaller software companies, Califano said.

Businesses are in a Catch-22 situation when it comes to reporting such incidents because they fear publicity that might cause shareholders and customers to flee, Califano said.

But he and Dooley agreed that it's better to report the incident—and request anonymity—than to let it go on. However, if law enforcement does investigate and finds your systems have been violated, you have no control over the publicity, they said.

Firewalls, intrusion detection software and file backups are all important—though not foolproof—protections against cybercrime, Dooley said.

Companies must also be wary of cybertheft from the inside, such as employees looking to cash in on a company's source code, Califano said.

Diligent prevention methods can minimize risk by about 90 percent, said John Breen, regional vice president for SBC DataComm, SBC Communications' cybercrime prevention unit.

For $235 per hour the company will assess a business' vulnerability and make recommendations, Breen said. SBC DataComm also offers a service to manage all of a client firm's security. That service runs about $2,700 a month for the first main site, Breen said.

The service keeps a company updated on the latest viruses and remedies, Breen said. "It's not a one-time fix and it's all over with," Breen said. "It's an ongoing effort."

To report cybercrime against your business, call Joe Dooley at (203) 777-6311. SBC DataComm can be reached at 1-800-448-1008.

16

Federal Law Enforcement and Cyber Crime

How Much Can the Department of Homeland Security Do About Cyberattacks?

David Strom

How much can the Department of Homeland Security do about cyberattacks?
(Business/Financial Desk)(computer worms and viruses, and measures to stop
them, have been seriously disrupting electronic commerce)

C AN Tom Ridge keep the homeland safe for Internet surfing?
  I started wondering last week after I got a call from a woman I did
not know. She claimed my computer was sending hers a bunch of virus-
infected messages. I did not do it—honest.

It was all one big head fake, by some anonymous software writer out in
cyberspace, whose malicious code was worming its way through countless
PC's on the Internet. The virus, called SoBig.F, used e-mail address books

Cox dealt with the Blaster attack. But many other Internet service providers could have done a better job of disseminating such information.

Corporate network administrators need to put in place policies that assume the internal network is no longer composed of trusted machines, and deploy their equipment accordingly. There are simply too many vectors for infection these days.

"Most home users felt that they didn't have to worry about security," Ms. MacDonald said. "Hopefully, these incidents have raised our level of awareness as users."

Maybe Mr. Ridge needs to add a couple of new color codes to indicate worm and virus attacks.

17

Federal Bureau
of Investigation

The FBI's Cyber-Crime
Crackdown

Simson Garfinkel

*The FBI's cyber-crime crackdown: on one side, teen hackers and corrupt employees; on
the other, the FBI's computer-crime-fighting units. Let the battles begin.*

To protect the classified information stored on her desktop computer,
Special Agent Nenette Day uses one of the most powerful tool on the
planet—an air gap.

Day points to an IBM ThinkPad resting on the table behind her desk.
"That computer is hooked up to the Internet," she says. "But if you break
into it, have a good time: there's no secret work on it."

Two meters away on her desk sits Day's other computer—a gray-and-
chrome mini-tower emblazoned with a red sticker proclaiming that its hard
drive is classified SECRET. "This," she says protectively, "holds my e-mail."
Day readily talks about the ThinkPad, describing how she got it as part of a
big purchase by the Federal Bureau of Investigation (FBI) a few years ago and
explaining that it's now somewhat out-of-date. And she happily shows off a
collectible action figure—still in its display box—a colleague brought back

from Belgium. It's a "cyberagent" with a gun in one hand and a laptop computer in the other. But if you let your eyes drift back to that red sticker and try to copy the bold, black words printed on it, Day will throw you out of her office.

Day belongs to the FBI's Boston Computer Crime Squad, one of 16 such units located throughout the United States. Each is composed of about 15 agents who investigate all manner of assaults on computers and networks—everything from lone-hacker to cyberterrorist attacks—with a dose of international espionage thrown in for good measure. Crimes range from Web site defacements and break-ins to so-called denial-of-service attacks, which prevent legitimate users from accessing targeted networks.

The Computer Crime Squads form the heart of the FBI's new Cyber Division. Created as part of the FBI's reorganization that followed September 11, the Cyber Division is the U.S. government's first line of defense against cybercrime and cyberterrorism. Its mission, said FBI Director Robert S. Mueller, when he appeared before the Senate Committee on the Judiciary last May, is "preventing and responding to high tech and computer crimes, which terrorists around the world are increasingly exploiting to attack America and its allies."

The emphasis on cybercrime is a big departure for the FBI. The bureau's agents traditionally got the most attention—and the biggest promotions—by pursuing bank robbers, kidnappers, and extortionists. J. Michael Gibbons worked on one of the FBI's very first computer-crime cases back in 1986; when he left the FBI in 1999, he was chief of computer investigations. "Frankly," says Gibbons, now a senior manager at KPMG Consulting in McLean, VA, "there was no great glory in the FBI on working computer investigation cases."

But that attitude is changing as Washington increasingly realizes that big damage can be inflicted on U.S. businesses through their computers and networks. Remember back in February 2000 when a massive denial-of-service attack shut down Web sites belonging to companies such as Yahoo!, eBay, and Amazon.com? It cost those companies literally millions of dollars in lost revenue. That attack, it turns out, was executed by a single high school student. Experts worry that a similar assault on the nation's electric utilities, financial sector, and news delivery infrastructure, could dramatically exacerbate the resulting confusion and possibly even the death toll of a conventional terrorist attack, if the two attacks were coordinated.

Even without the specter of terrorism, cybercrime is bleeding millions of dollars from businesses. Earlier this year, the Computer Security Institute surveyed 503 organizations: together, they reported $456 million dollars in damages due to attacks on their computers and networks over the past year, and more than $1 billion in damage over the previous six years. Those numbers—which are the closest thing that the computer establishment has to reliable figures for the incidence of computer crime—have climbed more than 20 percent since 2001.

Day's activities show that although the FBI, the nation's premier law-enforcement agency, is starting to come to terms with cybercrime, it still has a long way to go. Agents such as Day receive special training and have access to specialized tools (many of which the FBI refuses to discuss). Their equipment, if not always at the James Bond cutting edge, is no longer embarrassingly out-dated. On the other hand, the FBI's cybercrime squads are locked in a battle to keep current in the face of unrelenting technological change, and they are so short-staffed that they can investigate only a tiny fraction of the computer crimes that occur. Agents such as Day have served as only a small deterrent to hackers and high tech criminals bent on attacking a society that has become hopelessly dependent on its machines. But the deterrent is growing.

HOW TO CATCH A CYBERCROOK

The phone rings at the FBI Crime Squad and a "complaint agent" answers. Most calls are short, not too sweet, and not terribly satisfying for the person seeking help. "We get a lot of phone calls from people who say that somebody has hacked their home computer," says Day. Others report death threats delivered in online chat rooms.

Unsettling as such events are for the victims, most callers are told that there's nothing the FBI can do for them. For one thing, federal computer-crime statutes don't even kick in unless there is at least $5,000 damage or an attack on a so-called "federal interest computer"—a broad category that includes computers owned by the federal government, as well as those involved in interstate banking, communications, or commerce. In places especially rife with computer crime, like New York City, the intervention bar is even higher.

Even cases whose damages reach the threshold often die for lack of evidence. Many victims don't call the FBI right away. Instead, they try to fix their computers themselves, erasing their hard drives and reinstalling the operating system. That's like wiping fingerprints off the handle of a murder weapon: "If you have no evidence, we can't work it," says Day. And, of course, an attack over the Internet can originate from practically anywhere—the other side of the street or the other side of the world. "We can't do a neighborhood sweep and ask, 'Did you see anybody suspicious walking around here?'" she explains.

For many computer offenses, the FBI lacks not only solid evidence but even the knowledge that an incident has occurred at all. According to this year's Computer Security Institute survey, only about one-third of computer intrusions are ever reported to law enforcement. "There is much more illegal and unauthorized activity going on in cyberspace than corporations admit to their clients, stockholders, and business partners, or report to law enforcement" says Computer Security Institute director Patrice Rapalus.

Every now and then, however, all the ingredients for a successful case come together: a caller who has suffered a significant loss, undisturbed evidence, and a perpetrator who is either known or easily findable.

Day remembers a case from October 2000. The call came from the vice president of Bricsnet US, a software company in Portsmouth, NH. Bricsnet had just suffered a massive attack over the Internet. Somebody had broken into its systems, erased customer files, modified financial records, and sent e-mail to Bricsnet's customers, announcing that the company was going out of business.

When Day arrived on the scene she went quickly for what she hoped would be the key source of evidence: the log files. These are the routine records—the digital diary—computers retain about their actions. Computers can keep highly detailed logs: an e-mail server, for example, might track the "To" and "From" addresses, as well as the date, of every message it processes. Some computers keep no log files at all. Getting lucky; Day found that Bricsnet's log file contained the time of the attack and the Internet Protocol, or IP, address, of the attacker's computer.

Every address on the Internet is assigned to either an organization or an Internet service provider. In the Bricsnet case, the address belonged to a local service provider. Day issued a subpoena to that company, asking for the name of the customer "who had connected on this IP address" when the attack took place. This information came from the service provider's own log files.

It turned out that the offending address corresponded to a dial-up connection. Each time a subscriber dials in, the service provider's log files record the date, time, username, and the originating phone number. Within a week of launching the investigation, Day had fingered a likely suspect: Patrick McKenna, a help desk worker whom Bricsnet had fired on the morning of the first attack. McKenna was arrested, charged, and convicted under the Computer Fraud and Abuse Act. He was sentenced in June 2001 to six months in federal prison, followed by a two-year parole. He was also ordered to pay restitution for the damage he had caused, which the court determined to be $13,614.11.

MASKED MEN AND DEAD ENDS

Day's bust in the Bricsnet case was unusual for its speed and for the resulting conviction. That's because many crimes are perpetrated with stolen usernames and passwords. In the Bricsnet case, for instance, McKenna had broken into the company's computers using his former supervisor's username and password.

The key to cracking the Bricsnet case was caller ID and automatic number identification (ANI), two technologies more and more Internet service providers are using to automatically record the phone numbers of people dialing up their servers. When a crime is committed over a telephone line, this information is invaluable.

"I love ANI," says Day. "The last thing you want to do is show up at Joe Smith's house because some hacker has logged in using Smith's username and password." This tool, she says, "lets you know if you are on the right track. It has made a huge difference." Not all new telecommunications technologies are so helpful, though. Many recent computer attacks, for example, flow from the growing availability of always-on high-speed Internet connections. Attackers employ computer viruses and other programs to compromise users' home computers, and then they use the compromised computers as platforms for launching other attacks without the owners' knowledge. Even worse, an attacker can jump from system to system, forging a long chain that cannot be traced. Microsoft Windows typically does not keep logs of its activity. "A lot of our investigations have been stopped cold in their tracks because someone is trotting through one of those computers," Day says, referring to cable-modem-connected PCs that run vulnerable copies of Microsoft Windows 95.

Even caller ID and automatic number-identification information can be faked by a person who has control of a corporate telephone system with a certain kind of connection to the public telephone network. So far, faked caller ID hasn't been a problem—but that could change, too.

The Internet's cloak of anonymity has made fighting crime especially tough. It's almost as if there were booths outside banks distributing free ski masks and sunglasses to everybody walking inside. "Anonymity is one of the biggest problems for the FBI crime squads," former agent Gibbons says. He maintains that cybercriminals' ability to disguise their identities does more than just complicate investigations; it also makes attackers more aggressive and more willing to take chances and do damage.

"People act differently when they don't think that they are being held accountable for their actions," says Gibbons. For years, computer security experts have maintained that corrupt employees and former insiders—such as McKenna at Bricsnet—perpetrate the lion's share of computer crime. But Day's experience contradicts this prevailing wisdom. Today things are changing: according to Day, most cases she investigates involve outsiders who commit their crimes anonymously over the Internet—frequently from overseas. Day says she has traced some 70 percent of the attacks to foreign Internet addresses. Nevertheless, insiders still represent the bulk of her investigations as they represent the most damaging attacks.

In one case, Day says, she determined that a major break-in had originated at a cybercafe in a small town in Romania. Because computer hacking is not a crime in Romania, the local police offered no assistance. Seeking help elsewhere, she phoned the cafe itself and talked with its owner, who spoke fluent English. "The owner said he has a bunch of cyberhackers who come there, but this is Romania, and they pay cash," Day says.

The investigation was terminated.

ATTACK OF THE GROWNUPS

The media frequently portray the typical computer criminal as a disaffected male youth, a computer wizard who lacks social skills. In the archetypal scene, FBI agents conduct a predawn raid: with their guns drawn, they arrest a teenager while his horrified parents look on. And in fact, Day says that as recently as five years ago, juveniles made up the majority of the perpetrators she encountered. They were teenagers who broke into Web sites that had little security, and their digital crowbars were tools that they downloaded freely from the Internet. These kids made no attempt to hide their success. Instead, they set up their own servers on the penetrated computers, bragged to their friends, and left behind lots of evidence of their misdeeds.

But such attacks are no longer the most important cases that Day's office investigates. Recent years have brought "an interesting shift," she says. Now she sees attackers breaking into computers that are supposedly protected by firewalls and security systems. These perpetrators—virtually all of them adults—mount extremely sophisticated attacks. They don't brag, and they don't leave obvious tracks. "It's economic espionage," Day concludes.

It's not surprising that these cases are the hardest to crack, she says. One incident involved a suspect who had used a stolen credit card to purchase dial-up accounts at Internet service providers, specifically smaller providers that did not use caller ID or automatic number identification. He then proceeded to quietly break into thousands of computers. Day monitored the attacker for four months, trying to figure out who he was. "He was very good," she recounts. Then, in the middle of her investigation, the stolen credit card was canceled and the dial-up accounts were closed. "I was horrified," she says. The investigation fell apart, and the perpetrator is still at large.

Computer crime culprits defy stereotyping. One case that was successfully prosecuted—after a three-year investigation by the FBI—involved an assistant principal at a Long Island high school. The school administrator flooded the e-mail systems at Suffolk, James Madison, and Drexel universities with tens of thousands of messages, causing significant damage. In July 2001 the culprit, whose crimes carried punishments as high as a year in jail and $200,000 in fines, was sentenced to six months in a halfway house.

In the coming years the widespread adoption of wireless-networking technology will probably pose the biggest problem for the FBI cybercrime squad. These networks, based on the 802.11(b), or Wi-Fi, standard, let people use laptops and handheld computers as they move freely about their homes and offices. But unless additional protective measures are taken, wireless signals invariably leak beyond buildings' walls: simply lurking within the 100- to 300-meter range of a typical base station, an attacker can break into a network without even picking up a telephone or stepping onto the victim's property. "Many people who are moving to wireless as a cost-saving measure don't have any appreciation of the security measures they should employ," explains Special Agent Jim Hegarty, Day's supervisor.

And as the Boston cybercrime unit has discovered, wireless attacks are not just theoretical. The wireless network of one high tech company recently suffered a break-in. According to Hegarty, the attacker—an activist who was opposed to the company's product and management—literally stationed himself on a park bench outside the company's offices and over the course of several weeks, used the wireless network to "sniff" usernames and passwords of the company's president and other senior-level executives. The activist then used the information to break into the company's computers—again, making his entry through its wireless network. Armed with this illicit access, the attacker downloaded months of e-mail and posted it on the Web.

The e-mail contained confidential information about customers and their contracts. Once that became public, all hell broke loose. Some customers who discovered that they were paying higher rates than others demanded better deals; others canceled orders upon discovering that the vendor had been selling the same product to their competitors. Ultimately, the attacked company suffered more than $10 million in direct losses from the break-in. As wireless networks proliferate, attacks of this kind are likely to become more common, according to Hegarty. The advent of 802.11, he says, "is going to be a watershed event for us."

ALL IN A DAY'S WORK

When Technology Review first approached the FBI about interviewing an agent of the computer crime squad, the idea was to write about an agent's "average day." The public affairs manager at the FBI's Boston office nixed the idea: there are no average days for an FBI agent, she said. Indeed, Day says that one of the best things about her job is its endless variety.

"I might spend one day in trial preparation. I could spend an entire day milling through computer files doing evidence assessment. The next day I could be scheduled to testify in a trial. And last month I spent a couple weeks in Bangkok, Thailand, teaching police from 10 different Asian countries." She spends some days on the phone, perhaps overseeing a new case coming in from a financial institution or phoning FBI headquarters with information that needs to be relayed to other field offices. A few days later she might be off to the range for weapons training. Agent Day carries a .40-caliber Glock 23 and assists on the occasional drug raid. "It is very long work, and it's very hard," she says about her job, "but it gives you something that you would never see in the private sector."

The Glock doesn't get much use out there on the Internet, of course, but Day's FBI training in understanding criminal behavior does. She is, for example, involved in a project at the FBI's research center in Quantico, VA, developing a psychological profile of serial hackers—people who might become criminals or could be hired by a foreign government. A serial hacker could be a powerful tool for Al Qaeda or some other terrorist organization.

Moving forward, the biggest challenge, says Day, will be for society as a whole "to try to define and distinguish between what is basically online vandalism—when somebody is damaging a business or a computer—and cyberterrorism. All of those things are conflated in the discussion of the criminal prosecution of hackers. In my mind those are different kinds of contact with different social harm."

Today cybercrime is one of the FBI's top priorities—even above fraud, drugs, and gun running, says Day. But while scary talk of cyberterrorism captures the headlines, the most damaging cybercrime may actually be old-fashioned crimes being committed with new and virtually untraceable tools. Catching the new bad guys will require people like Nenette Day to stay on technology's leading edge, but it will also require an FBI able to build an organization that gives Day and her fellow agents adequate support. Furthermore, it will require the capability to bring superior computing firepower against the cyberattackers and beat them at their own high tech game.

RELATED ARTICLE: HALL OF CYBERINFAMY

John Draper, "Captain Crunch"

Crime: Draper discovered in 1972 that by blowing the whistle that came with Cap'n Crunch cereal, he could create the 2600-hertz tone necessary to seize control of telephone systems and place free long-distance phone calls.

Punishment: Draper was arrested in May 1972 for illegal use of telephone company property. He was put on probation, but in 1976 he was arrested again on wire fraud charges and spent four months in prison. While serving time, he started programming the EasyWriter word processor for the Apple II computer.

Kevin Mitnick

Crime: While in high school, Mitnick broke into computer systems operated by Digital Equipment Corp. and downloaded the source code to the operating system. By 1994 Mitnick was considered the federal government's most wanted computer hacker.

Punishment: Following a nationwide manhunt, Mitnick was arrested in February 1995 and held for four years without trial. Specific allegations were never published on the grounds of "national security." Mitnick was released from prison in January 2000 under a plea bargain.

Kevin Poulsen

Crime: A friend of Kevin Mitnick, Poulsen rigged Los Angeles radio call-in shows to guarantee that a pal would win a car giveaway. He also broke into the FBI's National Crime Information Center, downloading active case files and alerting suspects in undercover FBI investigations.

Punishment: Poulsen spent three years in prison for hacking and was forbidden to touch a computer for three additional years after his release. He is now a journalist, covering computer security for SecurityFocus, an online business service.

"Mafiaboy"

Crime: This Canadian juvenile was responsible for the February 2000 denial-of-service attacks on CNN, Yahool, E★Trade, and other major Web sites.

Punishment: Arrested in April 2000 by the Royal Canadian Mounted Police working in cooperation with the FBI, the youth, whose name was withheld because of his age, pled guilty to 56 counts of computer crime in January 2001. He was sentenced in September 2001 to eight months of "open custody" and one year probation, as well as restricted access to the Internet.

Onel De Guzman

Crime: In May 2000 the ILOVEYOU computer worm spread throughout the world as an e-mail attachment. Worldwide damage in lost productivity and clogged networks was estimated at $10 billion.

Punishment: The FBI quickly traced the worm to the Philippines and identified computer science student De Guzman as the perpetrator. Phillipine authorities brought charges against him but then dismissed the case in August 2000, saying that the country's laws did not cover computer crime.

18

The United States Secret Service

SS 1 E-Crime Squad

William Jackson

SS 1 E-crime squad: Secret Service goes where the crime is—into cyberspace. (Policy Alert).

The Secret Service, formed in 1865 to combat counterfeiting, has become the lead agency in investigating electronic crime.

It was a natural evolution, said Michael Stenger, special agent in charge of the Washington field office, because "the majority of counterfeit money in the United States today is produced on computers."

Not only has counterfeiting become high tech, but credit card fraud, check forgery and even threats against the president have all "gravitated to electronic media," Stenger said. "We had to develop the expertise to handle the investigations we are doing now."

Wayne Peterson, a member of the Washington office's Electronic Crimes Task Force, said, "Just about every search warrant we execute now involves a computer."

Even if a crime is not electronic in nature, computers frequently produce evidence for the investigation. About 100 agents across the country have been trained in computer forensics by the Secret Service's Electronic Crimes Special Agent Program.

The 2001 USA Patriot Act called for the Secret Service to establish a network of task forces, and Washington's is one of nine so far. The first came into being in the 1990s in New York because of online banking crimes.

Bankers "started calling their friends at the Secret Service," said Chris McFarland, assistant to the special agent in charge of the Washington office.

New York's model helped in setting up the Washington field office. Today its e-crimes task force includes law enforcement agencies from Baltimore to Richmond, Va., as well as organizations such as AOL Time Warner Inc. and Nextel Communications Inc.

The Washington office has 12 agents dedicated to the task force, five of them trained in forensics. Other task forces, all sharing information and resources, are near Boston, Charlotte, N.C., Chicago, Las Vegas, Los Angeles, Miami and San Francisco.

Cooperation among the task forces is a product of the Secret Service's small size. "Historically we have had good relations with other agencies," Stenger said.

Corporate cooperation with the task force usually is informal, but law enforcement agencies commonly sign a memorandum of understanding, McFarland said. Local departments might have an officer sworn in as a special federal deputy to ease investigations across jurisdictions. About 20 special deputies from local enforcement agencies work with the Washington task force.

The task forces can shift personnel or accept evidence for investigation as needed. "We've learned to be flexible and travel light," McFarland said.

The Washington office has two labs equipped with 10 custom forensic workstations with multiple hard drive bays from Skytek Inc. of Alexandria, Va., as well as two Apple Computer Inc. systems. Hard drives brought in as evidence must be mirrored before examination.

"If you touch a file [on a drive], you can change the date or time stamp, raising questions in court," Peterson said.

He left the Secret Service several years ago for the private sector but later returned. During the high-tech boom the money was good, "and I took the bait," he said. "But I always missed the service. I had mixed feelings." After the attacks on Sept. 11, 2001, he decided to come back.

SECURITY SURVEY SAYS . . .

Despite the growing volume of electronic crime, Peterson said, the workload is not too heavy. "It comes, and it goes," he said. He has developed a survey to help companies evaluate their network security—part of the outreach that is the task force's top priority.

"Prosecution is third on the list for us" behind education and prevention, McFarland said.

For several years, representatives from the service and other agencies, including the FBI and National Security Agency, have been making the rounds of conferences and trade shows, asking for private-sector cooperation. To combat e-crime, they say, companies must be willing to report incidents and share information with each other and with law enforcement.

So far, results have been mixed.

In a recent Salt Lake City talk, McFarland asked his audience how many had been victims of hacking. Almost everyone raised a hand. Asked how many had reported the incidents, almost no one raised a hand.

"It's a matter of relationships," McFarland said. Where relationships exist, cooperation is much better, he said. "The thing that worries me most now is the wireless networking that people are putting into their homes," because compromised home computers can become launching pads for attacks.

"The difference between physical and IT security is becoming less and less," he said.

19

Private Efforts to Combat Cyber Crime

A Key Weapon to Thwart Cybercrime

Alex Salkever

Highly publicized FBI busts are nice. What consumers really need, though, is timely information they can use to protect themselves. (NOTHING BUT NET)

On Nov. 20 the FBI announced a massive Internet crime bust. Dubbed Operation Cyber Sweep, the investigation netted 125 arrests and indictments over the course of seven weeks. The FBI says those arrested, indicted, and convicted are responsible for $100 million worth of crimes affecting 125,000 Americans and dozens of businesses. The busted ranged from crackpots to the purely craven, including a disgruntled baseball fan who allegedly hacked into the computers of the Philadelphia Phillies and a credit-card scamster charged with using bogus card numbers and bad checks to beat online electronics store Outpost.com out of $80,000 worth of merchandise.

In Operation Cyber Sweep, which is still ongoing, the FBI coordinated actions with dozens of law-enforcement agencies at the federal, state, and local level. Top FBI officials emphasized that the operation shows how high a

"A Key Weapon to Thwart Cybercrime" by Alex Salkever, *BusinessWeek,* Dec. 2, 2003. Reprinted by permission.

priority cybercrime is for bureau investigators, and clearly, the busts bumped the battle up several notches.

"Online criminals assume that they can conduct their schemes with impunity," said Attorney General John Ashcroft at a Nov. 20 press conference. "Operation Cyber Sweep is proving them wrong, by piercing the criminals' cloak of anonymity and prosecuting them to the fullest extent of the law."

FOLLOWING THE DOUGH

The FBI and its cohorts are to be lauded for the inroads they seem to be making in attacking cybercrime. But let's keep this in perspective. The folks who've been nabbed are mainly small-time confidence artists or at the most mid-level scamsters. The busted are the ones who could barely cover their tracks. And they resided in the U.S.—easy pickings as compared to, say, Indonesia, where the FBI would find it slightly more difficult to collar international cyberthieves.

Criminals rob banks because that's where the money is. Likewise, in cyberspace expect the most ingenious criminals to follow the dough. That hardly means penny-ante operations that pick off a handful of credit-card and bank-account numbers.

Rather, the big money is in the big databases. Credit-card companies, banks, and credit-reporting agencies all store most of the files they keep on hundreds of millions of people in these big data warehouses, which are far more heavily guarded than someone's password at an e-commerce site. Major corporations understand that these big databases are an enormous liability and deserve serious security firepower.

DANGEROUS MIGRATION

Inevitably, however, more and more of these supersensitive storehouses will suffer breaches. That's simply the law of large numbers as more and more people come online with broadband connections and more evil brains begin to comprehend the motherlode these data centers hold. A skilled malicious hacker could leverage a breach with other software to harvest personal IDs and export them en masse to any location around the globe. With that info they could apply for a million credit cards in a day or drain $5 out of millions of bank accounts—enough to get rich but not enough to raise an immediate alarm.

And a number of these big guys have already been hacked or suffered serious breaches ranging from unauthorized use of external access to their databases to suspicious break-ins that likely released hundreds of thousands of sensitive files into the cyber underground. Rarely are these databases connected directly to the public Internet, but then again supposedly neither were the ATM machines that failed under the barrage of bogus traffic when the Slammer worm struck in the summer of 2003.

What's more, many of these databases are rapidly moving offshore and, therefore, outside the easy reach of U.S. law enforcement. Two of the three big credit-reporting agencies say they intend to move significant portions of their operations overseas, according to a Nov. 7 article in the San Francisco Chronicle by investigative reporter David Lazarus. Many banks and credit-card companies did this a long time ago, meaning that Ma and Pa Kettle's credit report is as likely to be retrieved from Bombay as from Boston.

E-MAIL ALERTS

The upshot? While the FBI's Operation Cyber Sweep is necessary and should continue, it's only the first step—knocking down the low-hanging fruit—on a long path to better Internet data security. Another key step would be starting to build strong coalitions with law-enforcement agencies in the countries where these frauds will most likely take place. A series of high-profile busts overseas would carry more weight than anything that was done just stateside.

Equally key is to give consumers the tools they need to detect anything fishy in their accounts. Some financial institutions already offer capabilities such as e-mail notification of any suspicious credit-card activity. That's good and should be expanded.

Two of the three credit-reporting agencies offer an annual paid service that sends customers an e-mail anytime their credit history changes or is accessed. But the agencies claim they can't force any banks or other financial institutions to call individuals whose records have been pulled even if they have a fraud-alert warning on their credit file. And the cost of paying for both services separately is over $100 annually. The third credit-reporting agency continues to keep consumers in the dark when it comes to e-mail notification.

FAIR FIGHT

California has taken the more radical but equally welcome step of mandating that companies and organizations that get hacked notify potential victims as quickly as possible. That's unlikely to become a federal law anytime soon, and that's too bad. The public is the best defense against online fraud.

Yes, keep busting the bad guys both here and abroad. But the government really needs to give people what they need to fight this scourge: more information. A good start would be a unified system that would notify consumers whenever their credit file has been accessed at any of the big credit-reporting agencies. That could be run by the government or by a third-party nonprofit created for the task. The notifications could travel via e-mail or snail mail, depending on personal preferences.

While banks and credit-card companies have gone a long way toward correcting past problems with notifying and protecting customers, a California-style law with teeth is necessary on a national level. That would mean banks and other financial institutions would face the very real risk of civil penalties if they don't notify affected customers in a timely fashion.

AVERTING CATASTROPHE

At the very least, everyone should have the right to know that they may be at risk for the rest of their lives. This is particularly important as more fraudsters are now staggering their use of purloined information over months and even years to attract too much attention.

These steps won't address all Internet crime sectors. "Phishing," where online scam artists dupe people via clever e-mail into coughing up account and personal information can't be directly stopped by either measure. What they will do, however, is prevent an inconvenient breach from turning into a major catastrophe for Web surfers and the companies that sell to them.

With the right information in hand, consumers can look after their own best interests and serve as a far more potent mechanism than Operation Cyber Sweep to keep online fraud in check.

InfoMarks: Make Your Mark

What Is an InfoMark?

It's a single-click return ticket to any page, any result, any search from InfoTrac College Edition.

An InfoMark is a stable URL, linked to InfoTrac College Edition articles that you have selected. InfoMarks can be used like any other URL, but they're better because they're stable—they don't change. Using an InfoMark is like performing the search again whenever you follow the link—whether the result is a single article or a list of articles.

How Do InfoMarks Work?

If you can "copy and paste," you can use InfoMarks.

When you see the InfoMark icon on a result page, its URL can be copied and pasted into your electronic document—web page, word processing document, or email. Once InfoMarks are incorporated into a document, the results are persistent (the URLs will not change) and are dynamic.

Even though the saved search is used at different times by different users, an InfoMark always functions like a brand new search. Each time a saved search is executed, it accesses the latest updated information. That means subsequent InfoMark searches might yield additional or more up-to-date information than the original search with less time and effort.

Capabilities

InfoMarks are the perfect technology tool for creating:

- Virtual online readers
- Current awareness topic sites—links to periodical or newspaper sources
- Online/distance learning courses
- Bibliographies, reference lists
- Electronic journals and periodical directories
- Student assignments
- Hot topics

Advantages

- Select from over 15 million articles from more than 5,000 journals and periodicals
- Update article and search lists easily
- Articles are always full-text and include bibliographic information
- All articles can be viewed online, printed, or emailed
- Saves professors and students time
- Anyone with access to InfoTrac College Edition can use it
- No other online library database offers this functionality
- FREE!

How to Use InfoMarks

There are three ways to utilize InfoMarks—in HTML documents, Word documents, and Email

HTML Document

1. Open a new document in your HTML editor (Netscape Composer or FrontPage Express).
2. Open a new browser window and conduct your search in InfoTrac College Edition.
3. Highlight the URL of the results page or article that you would like to InfoMark.
4. Right click the URL and click Copy. Now, switch back to your HTML document.
5. In your document, type in text that describes the InfoMarked item.
6. Highlight the text and click on Insert, then on Link in the upper bar menu.
7. Click in the link box, then press the "Ctrl" and "V" keys simultaneously and click OK. This will paste the URL in the box.
8. Save your document.

Word Document

1. Open a new Word document.
2. Open a new browser window and conduct your search in InfoTrac College Edition.
3. Check items you want to add to your Marked List.
4. Click on Mark List on the right menu bar.
5. Highlight the URL, right click on it, and click Copy. Now, switch back to your Word document.
6. In your document, type in text that describes the InfoMarked item.
7. Highlight the text. Go to the upper bar menu and click on Insert, then on Hyperlink.

8. Click in the hyperlink box, then press the "Ctrl" and "V" keys simultaneously and click OK. This will paste the URL in the box.
9. Save your document.

Email

1. Open a new email window.
2. Open a new browser window and conduct your search in InfoTrac College Edition.
3. Highlight the URL of the results page or article that you would like to InfoMark.
4. Right click the URL and click Copy. Now, switch back to your email window.
5. In the email window, press the "Ctrl" and "V" keys simultaneously. This will paste the URL into your email.
6. Send the email to the recipient. By clicking on the URL, he or she will be able to view the InfoMark.